Lyric Time: Dickinson and the Limits of Genre

The Corporeal Self: Allegories of the Body
in Melville and Hawthorne

WRITING NATURE
Henry Thoreau's *Journal*

SHARON CAMERON

THE UNIVERSITY OF CHICAGO PRESS
Chicago and London

The University of Chicago Press, Chicago 60637
The University of Chicago Press, Ltd., London

98 97 96 95 94 93 92 91 90 89   5 4 3 2 1

Library of Congress Cataloging in Publication Data

Cameron, Sharon.
  Writing nature : Henry Thoreau's Journal / Sharon Cameron.
       p.   cm.
  Reprint. Originally published: New York : Oxford University Press,
c1985.
  Bibliography: p.
  Includes index.
  1. Thoreau, Henry David, 1817–1862. Journal.   2. Thoreau, Henry
David, 1817–1862. Walden.   3. Nature in literature.   I. Title.
PS3053.C296   1988   88-25163
818'.309—dc19   CIP
ISBN 0-226-09228-3 (pbk.)

We want a man to give us that which was most precious to him—not his life's blood but even that for which his life's blood circulated what he has got by living—

Journal 2: 1842–1846 (141)

Contents

Acknowledgments

Versions of chapter two were delivered as lectures at Harvard University, the University of Utah, the University of Illinois, and Yale University.

I am grateful to the John Simon Guggenheim Memorial Foundation and to The Johns Hopkins University for the resources that permitted the writing of this book. The Pierpont Morgan Library permitted quotation from the unpublished manuscripts of Thoreau's *Journal* it has in its holdings. Princeton University Press allowed me to quote from *Journal 1: 1837–1844*, ed. Elizabeth Hall Witherell et al. (Princeton: Princeton University Press, 1981), *Journal 2: 1842–1848*, ed. Robert Sattelmeyer (Princeton: Princeton University Press, 1984), and *Walden*, ed. J. Lyndon Shanley (Princeton: Princeton University Press, 1971). The Textual Center for the Writings of Henry D. Thoreau gave me access to, and permission to quote from, unpublished transcripts of the text they are establishing. Elizabeth Hall Witherell, Editor-in-Chief of the Thoreau Edition, answered questions about a consistent text, and, for the *Journal* years 1848 to April 27, 1852, checked the quotations.

I wish to thank Joan Burbick, who first introduced me to Thoreau's *Journal*, and the Thoreau critics whose just attention to Thoreau's other writings afforded me the leisure to focus on the *Journal*. I would especially like to thank Stanley Cavell for a useful conversation about *Walden* and the *Journal*. His book on *Walden*, though I argue with it, was important to my thinking.

Michael Warner prepared the manuscript and corrected its errors. Jonathan Crewe, Deborah Kaplan, Jane P. Tompkins, Barry Weller, Elizabeth Falsey, Barbara Harman, and William Cain read all or portions of the manuscript. Garrett Stewart and Eric Sundquist read the whole thing. And, again, read the whole thing. The book is several times transformed for the generosity of their ideas. Harvard University offered me an appointment as a Visiting Scholar in the Department of Psychology and Social Relations, where I was installed for eleven crucial months in an office in William James. Roger Brown oversaw this hospitality. He also made it possible.

Textual Note

Editors for *The Writings of Henry D. Thoreau,* at the University of California, Santa Barbara, are currently establishing a text for Henry Thoreau's *Journal.* Where their work is available either in published text—*Journal 1: 1837–1844,* ed. Elizabeth Hall Witherell et al. (Princeton: Princeton University Press, 1981) and *Journal 2: 1842–1848,* ed. Robert Sattelmeyer (Princeton: Princeton University Press, 1984)—or as transcripts of a manuscript for which the final edited text has not yet been established (from 1848 to April 27, 1852), I rely on it. From May 1, 1852 on, passages cited are from the edition published by Bradford Torrey and Francis H. Allen, *The Journal of Henry D. Thoreau* (Boston: Houghton Mifflin, 1906). This is less confusing than it initially seems, as the source and state of the text can be determined by the date of the passage cited. Thus newly edited published text exists until 1848; the Princeton edition transcripts until April 17, 1852; the Torrey and Allen edition for all subsequent citations. In my references, the first number indicates volume, the second the page. Page numbers in the Princeton edition transcripts are not related to Thoreau's pagination of the manuscript volumes; the transcript pages have been numbered continuously for the convenience of the editors. Volumes of the Princeton edition text are in arabic, of the Torrey and Allen, in roman numerals.

I wish to elaborate on the policy that dictates my quotation from the text based on transcriptions made at the Textual Center for *The Writings of Henry D. Thoreau* (the text for the years 1848 to April 27, 1852). Thoreau continued to work on passages in his *Journal* after initially entering them, revising them sometimes in pencil, sometimes in ink. When his intention for an added word or phrase is clear, either because he has cancelled the word or phrase in the line or used a caret to show the position, or because of the context and the sense of the sentence, I incorporate his interlineations. When the interlineation is not clear, or when he interlineates an alternate reading without specifying preference or position, I present the reading of the text that is on line in the manuscript. My aim throughout has been to represent the latest version of the text when the additions or interlineations are unambiguous. The punctuation in the quotations is that of Thoreau. The brackets in the text represent the transcriber's questions about Thoreau's handwriting. They are not Thoreau's.

WRITING NATURE

1

The Journal *Against* Walden: *A Preliminary Perspective*

For a period of twenty-four years Henry Thoreau wrote forty-seven manuscript volumes of a journal. The *Journal*, published in its entirety in 1906, reprinted twice and comprising two million words, is known to us through a fourteen-volume library edition.[1] Alternatively, the *Journal* is known to us from popular editions of homiletic sententiae garnered selectively from the whole work. Yet neither the library edition, nor the scholarly edition that will supersede it, nor finally the popular selections removed from their generating context has produced—or could produce—an adequate reader's edition. In the case of the whole *Journal*, general readers are inappropriately asked to assume a scholar's role in working through a mind-numbing amount of material. In the case of the exemplary fragments, statements are pried from their contexts, distorting the integrity of Thoreau's characteristic rethinkings and redefinitions. The result of alternatives too compendious or too fragmentary is that Thoreau's *Journal*—the great nineteenth-century American meditation on nature—remains, to this day, inaccessible to the general reader. Yet notwithstanding the absence of an adequate text, and the problems which I shall suggest attend its representation, notwithstanding the dearth of critical commentary, we know that Thoreau came to think of the *Journal* as his central literary enterprise.

The *Journal* spans the years between 1837 and 1861,[2] during which time—to reiterate the chronology produced by Walter Harding[3]—Thoreau opened a private school (1838); delivered his first lecture at the Concord Lyceum (1838); travelled to the

3

Maine Woods (1838, 1846, 1853, 1857) and, with his brother John, down the Concord and Merrimack Rivers (1839); contributed pieces to the *Dial* (1840–44); witnessed the death, from lockjaw, of his brother, John (1842); tutored William Emerson's children on New York's Staten Island (1843); accidentally set fire to the Concord Woods (1844); built his Walden cabin, and, on Independence Day, moved in (1845); moved away from Walden Pond (1847) to live for another year at the Emersons', until he returned to his father's house (1848); published "Ktaadn and the Maine Woods" (1848) and *A Week on the Concord and Merrimack Rivers* (1849); travelled to Cape Cod (1849, 1850, 1855), saw the publication of *Walden* (1854), lectured on slavery (1854); worked as a surveyor (1856); was introduced to Walt Whitman (1856); visited the White Mountains (1858); delivered "The Succession of Forest Trees" at the Middlesex Cattle Show (1860); left for Minnesota with Horace Mann, Jr., hoping a change of place would affect his failing health (1861); returned after less than two months to Concord, Massachusetts, where he lived until May 6, 1862.[4]

The *Journal* remains essentially dumb about the details of these exploits. In fact, it appears that Thoreau is not supplementing his experience as the chronology describes it, but that he is writing his life so that it actually comes to comprise alternate—natural—phenomena. On October 25, 1857, Thoreau will write: "These regular phenomena of the seasons get at last to be—they were *at first*, of course—simply and plainly phenomena or phases of my life. The seasons and all their changes are in me" (X:127). Even once we establish, however, that the heart of Thoreau's *Journal* is its meditations on nature, discovering a vocabulary with which to discuss the *Journal* is no easy task. As I shall suggest in the following pages, the *Journal* itself prohibits the use of many interpretive procedures ordinarily taken for granted. Returning one night from a walk in the moonlight, Thoreau notes with satisfaction: "This light & this hour takes the civilization all out of the landscape—" (September 5, 1851 [7:74]). The same could be said of Thoreau's *Journal* itself because of the monotony of a record which focuses for twenty-four years on cyclical change; because of the plotlessness and discontinuity of the story of that change (the

thread of coherence being the repetition of the seasons); because of the progressive refusal to interpret the observations
recorded, as if the significance of the description of a tree were
the description of that tree; because of how minimally human
contacts are noted in the *Journal*. The people who appear are
represented by unelaborated names, like that of the farmer
Minott who lives nearby; or by initials (C. for Channing, the
poet-naturalist who accompanies Thoreau on his walks); or by
references to the unspecified "friend" whose presence in the
Journal is nonetheless recurrent. Elsewhere, friends are represented by blanks—by calculated omissions—as if Thoreau
wishes to preserve a given observation and to dislocate it from
the person who has generated it: "_____ is too grand for me
He belongs to the nobility & wears their cloak & manners—is
attracted to Plato not to Socrates—" (January 31, 1852 [9:480]).

Moreover, the meditations give the disconcerting double impression of commanding attention and of being random. We
could attribute this randomness to the genre of journal-writing.
Though after June 1851 entries occur almost every day, they
have no consistent length. There is also a division between one
entry and another[5] and between sequential subjects in the same
entry, whose relationship seems additive rather than develop-
mental. Yet the randomness we notice not only seems a product
of journal discourse; it also seems cultivated. "Perhaps I can
never find so good a setting for my thoughts as I shall thus have
taken them out of" (January 28, 1852 [9:460]), Thoreau insists,
and what he means to stress is that the integrity of a vision
depends upon its placement in a context at once primary and
unstructured, an integrity which any second, ordered context—
any reconstruction—violates. Nature is the first setting out of
which he doesn't wish to take his thoughts. The second setting,
as he tells us on January 27, 1852, is the *Journal*:

I do not know but thoughts written down thus in a journal might be
printed in the same form with greater advantage—than if the related
ones were brought together into separate essays. They are now allied
to life—& are seen by the reader not to be far fetched— It is more
simple—less artful— I feel that in the other case I should have no
proper frame for my sketches. Mere facts & names & dates communicate more than we suspect— (9:459–460)

The passage I have just cited occurs only one day after Thoreau records in his *Journal* the sentences memorialized by *Walden:* "What if all the ponds were shallow! would it not react on the minds of men? If there were no physical deeps. I thank God that he made this pond deep & pure—for a symbol. . . . While men believe in the infinite some ponds will be thought bottom- less" (January 26, 1852 [9:451]). Though Thoreau will transfer the observation to *Walden,* on January 28, 1852, he nonetheless insists on the priority of the *Journal* context: "Where also will you ever find the true cement for your thoughts? How will you ever rivet them together without leaving the marks of the file?" (9:460). We shall see how the wholeness of nature and the wholeness of the *Journal* will come to be identical.

Yet Thoreau's idea of totality is, as I have been suggesting, predicated not on connections but on the breaking of connec- tions. In fact, discontinuity could be described as the *Journal's* dominant feature, for no thought is ever entirely separated from or jointed to any other thought. On March 24, 1857, Thoreau himself stressed the relation between partiality, con- tingency, and consequent unity: "If you are describing any occurrence . . . make two or more distinct reports at different times . . . We discriminate at first only a few features, and we need to reconsider our experience from many points of view and in various moods in order to perceive the whole" (IX:300– 301). Again, underlining the fragmentary nature of the ven- ture, on February 3, 1859, he had noted: "The writer has much to do even to create a theme for himself. . . . It is only when many observations of different periods have been brought to- gether that he begins to grasp his subject and can make one pertinent and just observation" (XI:439).

One of the difficulties of regarding the *Journal* as draft mate- rial for *Walden* or for Thoreau's other writings (this is the way it is customarily considered) is that such a view fails to see the ways in which, though used for the published writings, the *Journal* is not, in fact, a version of the same enterprise, either inferior or superior to it, but attempts something different. One could, of course, say that the *Journal* is a book to which *Walden* is a prelude; that as the structure of *A Week* is composed of the days of a week, and the structure of *Walden* of the months of a year, so the structure of the *Journal* is composed of the years of a life. Yet though the *Journal* does take up more time than the previous books, it also cuts across the temporal units on which those books' meaning rests. As the following passage of February 27, 1851, suggests, it seeks to discover alternative orders of significance:

> Walking in the woods it may be some afternoon the sh[ad]ow of the wings of a thought flits across the landscape of my mind And I am reminded [how] little eventful is our lives What have been all these wars & survivors of wars and modern discoveries & improvements so called a mere irri[t]ation in the skin. But this shadow which is so soon past & whose substan[ce] is not detected suggests that there are events of importance whose interval is to us a true historic period. (5:380)

If in the previous passage thought is an event that converts the mind to a landscape against which temporal phenomena are trivialized, the following passage from July 21, 1851, moves beyond recognizable phenomena entirely, where nothing predetermined obstructs the clear line of vision:

Now I yearn for one of those old meandering dry uninhabited roads which lead away from towns—which lead us away from temptation, which conduct to the outside of earth—over its uppermost crust— where you may forget in what country you are travelling—where no farmer can complain that you are treading down his grass—no gentleman who has recently constructed a seat in the country that you are trespassing—on which you can go off at half cock—and waive adieu to the village—along which you may travel like a pilgrim—going nowhither. Where travellers are not too often to be met. Where my spirit is free—where the walls & fences are not cared for—where your head is more in heaven than your feet are on earth—which have long reaches—where you can see the approaching traveller half a mile off and be prepared for him—not so luxuriant a soil as to attract men— some root and stump fences which do not need attention—where travellers have no occasion to stop—but pass along and leave you to your thoughts— Where it makes no odds which way you face whether you are going or coming—whether it is morning or evening—mid noon or mid-night— Where earth is cheap enough by being public. Where you can walk and think with least obstruction—

there being nothing to measure progress by. Where you can pace when your breast is full and cherish your moodiness. Where you are not in false relations with men—are not dining nor conversing with them. By which you may go to the uttermost parts of the earth— It is wide enough—wide as the thoughts it allows to visit you. Sometimes it is some particular half dozen rods which I wish to find myself pacing over—as where certain airs blow then my life will come to me methink—like a hunter I walk in wait for it. When I am against this bare promontory of a hucklebery hill then forsooth my thoughts will expand. Is it some influence as a vapor which exhales from the ground, or something in the gales which blow there or in all things there brought together agreeably to my spirit? The walls must not be too high imprisoning me—but low with numerous—gaps. The trees must not be too numerous nor the hills too near bounding the view— nor the soil too rich attracting the attention to the earth— It must simply be the way and the life. (6:592–594)

Three pages later, still in the same entry:

In roads the obstructions are not under my feet—I care not for rough ground or wet even—but they are in my vision & in the thoughts or associations which I am compelled to entertain I must be fancy free— I must feel that wet or dry high or low it is the genuine surface of the planet & not a little chip dirt or a compost heap—or made land or redeemed. (6:597)

Six pages later, still in the same entry:

Remember thy creator in the days of thy youth. i. e. Lay up a store of natural influences— (6:603)

Although distractions keep returning Thoreau to the limits of the social world, the illusion of the passage is that when he breaks free he will walk "the genuine surface of the planet." The *Journal*, then, suggests that when familiar sights have been left behind, the man observing nature will not see with more nuance, but in the numerous gaps ("The walls must not be too high imprisoning me—but low with numerous—gaps. The trees must not be too numerous nor the hills too near bounding the view") he will see something different.

Perhaps such attempts to redefine vision by making it literally contingent upon nature ("When I am against this bare promontory of a huckleberry hill then forsooth my thoughts will expand"), with their attendant dismissals and accompanying dislocations, account for the fact that while it often seems easy to assign meaning to an excerpted journal passage, that same passage, returned to the journal context, presents us with not simply different foci, but ones which appear to be hierarchically competitive. In other ways, moreover, we see that the conventions through which we customarily specify our relation to texts or make claims about their meaning are, with respect to Thoreau's *Journal*, improperly distorting. I shall elaborate this observation later with respect to the issues raised by the reading of individual passages, and the presumptions they generate. At the moment, however, I wish to comment upon the way in which the distortion of perspective seems to govern our reading of the whole work.

When we train observation on single passages (as I do in the first two chapters) we appear to see the work too close-up. When we attempt to understand the properties of the *Journal* as a whole (as I do in the last two chapters) we feel at a speculative remove from it in which details have been sacrificed. I would suggest that our practices and expectations are made to seem inadequate from two points of view that are generated by the work itself, for an attempt to bring the two perspectives into alliance belies the alien sense of the *Journal* enterprise, which presents us simultaneously with incompatible foci: piecemeal observations in which man, not one with natural phenomena, unsuccessfully strains toward them; and, conversely, a disarming totality—forty-seven manuscript volumes which add up to nothing if not to a record of man's harmony with nature. Thus the very incongruity which disconcerts us about our perspective of the *Journal*, and about Thoreau's perspective *in* the *Journal* (so that we see the part without the whole or the whole without the part, the tear that will not allow us to put part and whole together) creates that requisite gap in which Thoreau will erect creations of another order. As if signalling these revisions, and prompting us to question them, a significant portion of the *Journal*'s passages are explicitly interrogative. Therefore, although when I consider a passage it may seem as if I am asking rhetorical questions to which I know the answers, in the *Journal*, as I shall explain in a moment, questions are integral to the meaning of passages which often seem at once catechistic and confusing. It might have been strategic to conduct my discussion as if this were not the case, but the fact is that the unsettling of perspective—specifically by raising the question of how part of a phenomenon is related to the whole of that phenomenon or to another phenomenon—is not just the *Journal's* practice; it is often the *Journal's* subject.

The *Journal* does, however, provide hints about interpreting its meaning, first, as I have noted, by making statements consistently interrogative, and therefore by suggesting that to understand the work we must keep their interrogative form intact; secondly, by composing the *Journal* discourse of what Thoreau variously calls "pictures" and "views." Here we might add the word "illustrations" to describe what the *Journal* anthologizes, for as the idea of serially collected "pictures" and "views" (which aspire to the formation of a composite whole) implies, renditions of a natural phenomenon exemplify its aspects. The *Journal* further insists that illustrations of nature are tainted by, and made to participate in, the questions that surround them. This is true partly because questions and illustrations are often syntactically inseparable. It is true partly because the very impulse to continue regarding a single landscape—to record multiple instances of it—implies questions about its meaning. I therefore understand Thoreau's propensity to ask questions, to see the landscape as a series of pictures, and to regard pictures as potential illustrations (of what, it is unclear) to be related. In a series of remarks, Thoreau will himself speculate that nature is a text whose interpretation requires readings of disparate aspects of it. On July 13, 1851, "I think how the history of the hills would read—since they have been pastured by cows—if every plowing & mowing & sowing & chopping were recorded" (6:567). On March 21, 1853, he asks, "Might not my Journal be called 'Field Notes?' " (V:32) And on July 8, 1851: "I am struck by the cool juicy pickled cucumber green of the potatoe fields now— How lusty these vines look. . . . Who can write the history of these fields?" (6:551–552). In this question, which I do take to be rhetorical, the implicit answer is "*I* can"—can write what Thoreau had designated as a "Natural *history* in a new sense" (August 21, 1851 [7:11]).

To that end, the *Journal*'s investigations may be epistemological, as in a passage I consider in the third chapter, which asks: "a meadow & an island; what are these things?" (4:285). Or they may ask about natural cause and effect. Of a windy day: "What does it mean. . . . ? Do plants & [tree] need to be thus tried & twisted? Is it a first intimation to the sap to cease to ascend—to thicken their stems?—" (7:23). Reconciling the two concerns, Thoreau may inquire about the duration for which man, to know nature, must be alert to its processes: "But this habit of close observation—In Humboldt—Darwin & others. Is it to be kept up long—this science—" (July 23, 1851 [6:617]). Or he may inquire about the metaphysical principles behind what the eye sees: "As I was riding to the ministerial Lot this morning about 8 ½ Am I observed that the white clouds in the west were disposed ray wise in the W and also in the east as if the sun's rays had split & so arranged them? A striking symetry in the heavens. What its law?" (8:301).

Although Thoreau tries frequently to discern "the laws, perchance, by which the world was made . . . seen in full operation in a rill of melted snow" (March 16, 1858 [X:299]), important passages of the *Journal* raise questions which resist the very answers that apparently are requisite: "These expansions of the river skim over before the river itself [takes] on its icy fetters. What is the analogy?" (4:291). As the latter instance, bereft of an answer, illustrates, Thoreau consistently refuses to anthropocentrize what he sees. While my categorical assertion requires the qualification of the following pages (including a more ample discussion of the passage just cited), I mean to stress the fact that in Thoreau's *Journal* the central Romantic question—"What is man's relation to the nature that he sees?"—undergoes drastic revision. One of the disconcerting features of the *Journal* is how thoroughly it dismisses not just Thoreau's consideration of himself but his consideration of other selves. What remains is just enough of the human to represent the natural: an isolated man recording his impressions of nature. Thus, while sentences that appear to rely on the pathetic fallacy infrequently occur in the *Journal,* as my fourth chapter elaborates, in this work which writes human beings virtually out of the picture and makes them literally marginal, there is no way, contextually, these passages could be considered anthropocentric. Given that fact, Thoreau's questions prompt our own. If a lifelong inquisition of nature is not meant to anthropomorphize what is seen, what is it meant to do?

I shall argue that Thoreau's attendance to the landscape—to borrow his own textual metaphor from the sentences about the icy river—is an effort to read it. Inadvertently addressing the task at which he labors, he writes: "There would be [this] advantage in travelling in your own country even in your own neighborhood, that you would be so thoroughly prepared to understand what you saw—" (June 12, 1851 [5:488]). Elaborating, on November 7, 1855: "My thoughts are concentrated; I am all compact. The solitude is real, too, for the weather keeps other men at home. This mist is like a roof and walls over and around. . . . I am *compelled* to look at near objects" (VIII:14). Sometimes the near object is part of the landscape through which the whole is framed: "Most trees are beautiful when leafing out, but especially the birch. . . . The birch leaves are so small that you see the landscape through the tree . . ." (May 17, 1852 [IV:62]). Elsewhere a single natural phenomenon, light on Walden Pond, is scrutinized intensively:

About 6:20 P.M. paddled on Walden . . . At first the sky was completely overcast, but, just before setting, the sun came out into a clear space in the horizon and fell on the east end of the pond and the hillside, and this sudden blaze of light on the still very fresh green leaves was a wonderful contrast with the previous and still surrounding darkness . . . while I in the middle was in the shade of the east woods—up under the verdure of the bushes and trees on the shore and on Pine Hill, especially to the tender under sides and to the lower leaves not often lit up. Thus a double amount of light fell on them, and the most vivid and varied shades of green were revealed. I never saw such a green *glow* before. The outline of each shrub and tree was a more or less distinct downy, or silvery crescent, where the light was reflected from the under side of the most downy, or newest, leaves,— as I should not have seen it at midday. . . .(August 28, 1860 [XIV:65])

If the previous passage implicitly assesses differences of light seen contrastively through the whole day, the following passage defines the light, conversely, by a circumscription of focus:

> the few varieties of wild pears here have more color and are handsomer than the many celebrated varieties that are cultivated. . . . I hold in my hand a Bonne Louise which is covered with minute brown specks or dots one twelfth to one sixteenth [of an inch] apart . . . . Each of these little ruptures, so to call them, is in form a perfect star with five rays; so that, if the apple is higher-colored, reflecting the sun, on the duller surface of this pear the whole firmament with its stars shines forth. . . . Looking through a more powerful glass, those little brown dots are stars with from four to six rays,—commonly five,—where a little wart-like prominence (perhaps the end of a pore or a thread) appears to have burst through the very thin pellicle and burst it into so many rays. (October 11, 1860 [XIV:113–115])

I have noted Thoreau's disinclination to anthropocentrize what he sees, and the metaphoricity of the previous passage therefore requires comment, for the rays of light on the pear are of course ways of indicating its blotches. The point of metaphor here, as I shall have occasion to remark later with respect to other passages, is not to compare natural and human worlds, but rather to expand the domain of the former, to insist on nature's infinite self-referentiality. Hence in the space marked by an ellipsis in the passage cited above, Thoreau will remark: "Pears, it is truly said, are less poetic than apples" (114). But concern with what is poetic immediately gets subsumed in the concentration on details with which the passage concludes and to which its metaphoric forays are subordinated. The ultimate goal of the comparison is not to connect pears to stars—with the comparison inaugurating a transcendence of the natural—but, as earlier sentences in the passage suggest, to connect pears to apples, pears to pears, pears to leaves, with comparison inaugurating a reiteration of the natural. Thus the purpose of metaphor seems here redefined, for the metaphor demonstrates the gratuitousness of transcendence rather than its desirability:

the few varieties of wild pears here have more color and are handsomer than the many celebrated varieties that are cultivated. The cultivated are commonly of so dull a color that it is hard to distinguish
them from the leaves, and if there are but two or three left you do not
see them revealing themselves distinctly at a distance amid the leaves,
as apples do, but I see that the gatherer has overlooked half a dozen
large ones on this small tree, which were concealed by their perfect
resemblance to the leaves,—a yellowish green, spotted with darker-
green rust or fungi (?). Yet some have a fair cheek, and, generally, in
their form, they are true pendants, as if shaped expressly to hang
from trees. (XIV:113)

It is in a context in which one aspect of nature is juxtaposed
to another aspect of nature (pears to apples, pears to pears,
pears to stars, pears to leaves) that the figure of rays of stars to
indicate blotches on pears must be understood. For while metaphor strictly defined is speech in which a word that denotes
one object is used to refer to another object, the point of that
crossing is customarily to establish its human significance; not
so in this case, where the presence of metaphor is muted by
details whose scientifically precise status it seems employed to
accentuate.

My reader will have noticed that my examples from the *Journal* text have been dominantly visual. This is not coincidence,
and however the following dichotomy may seem to stylize the
two texts, it is correct to note that while in *Walden* Thoreau is
concerned with the discovery of sound (so the commonplace
accurately expresses it), in the *Journal* he explores the complexi-
ties of vision. Hence the examples above (of light on the pond
and light on the pear) or of "the light of June" reflected from
"the under sides of the leaves" (IV:115) are not random, but
represent concerns which become progessively dominant from
1850 to 1861. The *Journal* text does not just compile disparate
sights, but also investigates what it means to transpose a visual
to a verbal medium. Consonant with Thoreau's interest in focus, composition, perspective and illustration, he importantly
distinguishes between observation, which anticipates what it
hopes to find, and seeing, for which no expectation can prepare one. Stating his preference: "I wish to see the earth
through the medium of much air or heaven" (September 12,

1851 [7:114]). Not alternatives, "air" and "heaven" are syno-
nyms for each other; the sentence concludes: "for there is no
paint like the air."

Despite the allusion to paint, and despite his indefatigable
dedication to observation and seeing, Thoreau rarely speaks—
or speaks well—of the visual arts, and as a consequence we
have no adequate idea of what paintings he would have seen.
Thoreau has a stake in disavowing visual compositions, for his
own composition—the *Journal*—is an alternative to a visual
medium.[6] The *Journal* draws on words to render landscapes
(specifically their changes) that Thoreau, I infer, faults paintings for making static. On November 3, 1861, in his last *Journal*
entry, I take Thoreau to be commenting on his own word-
painting without which "all this," though "perfectly distinct to
an observant eye," could yet "easily pass unnoticed" (XIV:346).
A year before, on November 28, 1860, as if forestalling the
obliviousness against which the *Journal* keeps its record, he had
written: "Let us make distinctions, call things by their right
names." The illustrations in the *Journal* follow these directives.
That questions should overtake statements; that declarative
sentences should seem interrogative (because their content
suggests uncertainty about what is being regarded; because
Thoreau cannot discern the focus that would organize a vision's elements; or simply because they are contaminated by
surrounding questions); that a consideration of single passages
and a consideration of the whole project should seem incompatible; that, as I shall suggest, subjects and illustrations
should appear inseparable from each other; that visual and
literary concerns should be made coordinates—these are not
features of all journal discourse. They are rather particular features of Henry Thoreau's *Journal*. They become rhetorical
strategies for what is, in effect, an anatomy of (seeing) nature,
as, with unacknowledged audacity, it transforms random
"field notes" to "a history of these fields."

In examining the discontinuities and categorical revisions I
have touched on above, I hope to open the *Journal* for public
scrutiny. In the following pages I do this progressively, moving
from issues that are verbal (from a consideration of the *Journal*'s
linguistic strategies, discussed in the next two chapters) to

issues that are auditory (to a consideration of who is meant to hear these words, discussed in the fourth chapter) to considerations that are professional (to the question of how we are to treat this material, discussed in the fifth chapter)—specifically I examine there theoretical issues instigated by problems of excerpting passages from the *Journal*. So doing, I suggest that the *Journal* raises questions of relation, and the representation of relation, in a number of contexts. It asks us to consider the relation between nature and the mind, and, alternatively, between aspects of a so-called single entity—the landscape seen through the birch trees by which it is therefore framed—that is, between one part of nature and another part of nature, to which it is juxtaposed. It asks us to consider Thoreau's relation to an audience for the *Journal* speculations, and to consider, as well, our relation *as* that audience to subjects which are made conventionally unavailable to us. In each of these cases, I argue that Thoreau presents us with discontinuities (between nature and the self, between one part of nature and another, between a clear assessment of what this work is—a private writer's journal—and a confusion about how to treat the *Journal* when it baffles the distinction between private and public). It is because critics have considered the *Journal* as fragmentary and private, not as a discrete entity, that it has not occurred to them to examine it as an autonomous composition. Because the work is a journal and because it was published posthumously, we assess it to be private. Yet claims made in the *Journal* explicitly about it—and in fact the nature of its composition—rather suggest that Thoreau hoped for our eventual discovery and assessment of this work *qua* work. Thus I shall argue the *Journal* confounds the distinction between the private and the public on which our determinations about how to treat discourse conventionally depend.

The question of how to treat discourse—in this case, how to quote or excerpt it—is central to my study not simply in practical terms (how do I make this material available to my reader?), but also in theoretical terms, for in the case of Thoreau's *Journal,* fragmentations in the text (partializations of subjects) and fragmentations of the text (quotations that represent those subjects) are related to each other. Thus I shall be suggesting that an inquiry into the *Journal* is primarily an investigation of how fragments epitomize relations (Thoreau's to nature, Thoreau's to an audience, journal discourse to published discourse, subjects to their exemplification). It is the premise of my study, then, that the *Journal* raises the problem of discontinuity in a number of contexts (suggesting that it exists between the self and a social world, between the self and nature, between the self and an audience); that these discontinuities are epitomized by the problem of fragmented or partially hidden communications; that the communications (the quotations I shall examine) are an emblem for, and often themselves thematically consider, relations that are simultaneously partialized and only partially visible. Although my fifth chapter discusses the problem of quotation in the context of Thoreau's own attempt to delineate an unstable relationship between parts and their representative wholes, since the issue of exemplification is, as I have indicated, central to the problem posed by the *Journal* and to my interest in considering it, in the remaining introductory pages I anticipate that discussion.

Because journals, in general, do not have continuous narratives, and because this journal exploits that fact, we have to construct connections between its various subjects, and this involves knowing which passages to read against which other passages. It also involves intuiting whether in the posing of repetitive questions or concerns a statement is being made. Yet the passages on which one focuses or which one contrasts will not reveal the *Journal's* argument; they will determine the argument, will determine the reader's conception of the whole work. Thus, for example, in *Consciousness in Concord* (in his "Introduction" to a so-called "lost year" of the *Journal*) Perry Miller, working with dissevered manuscript pages, suggests that the following passages—which he speculates were written prior to 1845—while not connected to each other, occur in the same entry:

Is there such virtue in raking cranberries that those men's employment whom I now see in the meadow can rightly reprove my idleness? Can I not go over these same meadows after them & rake still more valuable fruits—rake with my mind? Can I not rake a thought perchance which shall be worth a bushel of cranberries? . . .

It is pathetic for one far in the fields in mid [*word obscure*] to hear the village clock striking. The bees in the flowers [seem to (*pencil insertion*)] reprove my idleness yet I ask myself to what end do they labor? Is there so much need of honey & wax? Is the industry of mankind truly respectable? [(*crossed out:*) Can it rightly reprove my idleness?] I will not mind the village clock. It makes time for the dead & dying. It sounds like a knell; as if one struck the most sonorous slates in the churchyard with a mallet, & they rang out the words which are engraved on them—tempus fugit irrevocabile. I harken for the clock that strikes the eternal hours. What though my walk is [*word obscure*] and I do not find employment which satisfies my hunger & thirst, and the bee probing the thistle & loading himself with honey & wax seems better employed than I, my idleness is better than his industry. I would rather that my spirit hunger & thirst than that it forget its own wants in satisfying the hunger & thirst of the body.

I would fain hunger & thirst after life forever & rise from the present enjoyment unsatisfied. I feel the necessity of treating myself with more respect than I have done—of washing myself more religiously in the ponds & streams if only for a symbol of our inward cleansing & refreshment—of eating and drinking more abstemiously and with more discrimination of savors—recruiting myself for new and worthier labor. There are certain things which only senses refined and purified may take cognizance of— May such senses be mine! O that I might truly worship my own body as the worthiest temple of God— bow down with reverence to his image graven in it—& so love and reverence the very persons of my friends. May I love and revere myself above all the gods that men have ever invented, and never let the vestal fire go out in my senses.[7]

The first passage, however, (marked by the ellipsis) according to the Princeton editors, was written not prior to 1845 but on September 7, 1851. As I understand it, it does not espouse the superiority of idleness to profit (Miller's interpretation) but, as I shall suggest when I consider the passage in chapter two, rather inquires whether cranberries and thoughts may be equated with each other so as to be discussed on the same ground. In the Princeton transcript for that same entry, the passage about the bees does not *follow* the passage about cranberries; it *precedes* that passage. More to the point, the text

Perry Miller cites and the one the Princeton editors cite are not in fact the same. The Princeton transcript reads as follows:

How to live— How to get the most life! as if you were to teach the young hunter how to entrap his game. How to extract its honey from the flower of the world. That is my every day business. I am as busy as a bee about it. I ramble over all fields on that errand and am never so happy as when I feel myself heavy with honey & wax. I am like a bee searching the live long day for the sweets of nature. Do I not impregnate & intermix the flowers produce rare & finer varieties by transfering my eyes from one to another? I do as naturally & as joyfully with my own humming music—seek honey all the day. With what honied thought any experience yields me I take a bee line to my cell. It is with flowers I would deal. Where is the flower there is the honey—which is perchance the nectareous portion of the fruit—there is to be the fruit—& no doubt flowers are thus colored & painted—to attract & guide the bee. So by the dawning or radiance of beauty are we advertised where is the honey & the fruit of thought of discourse & of action— We are first attracted by the beauty of the flower, before we discover the honey which is a foretaste of the future fruit. Did not the young Achilles (?) spend his youth learning how to hunt? The art of spending a day. If it is possible that we may be addressed—it behoves us to be attentive. If by watching all day & all night—I may detect some trace of the Ineffable—then will it not be worth the while to watch? Watch & pray without ceasing. . . . I am convinced that men are not well employed—that this is not the way to spend a day. (7:82–83)

It may be that the passage cited by Miller is a draft for the entry reproduced by the Princeton text. If so, the disparity between the two passages would indicate the codification of a thought that, not untypically in the process of revision, arrives at its clarification by reversing rather than underlining the thrust of its original meaning: self-glorification becomes glorification of nature. Yet however we account for the discrepancies, to read Miller's passage is to be struck by Thoreau's narcissism (so Miller remarks: "Comment is mute before such declamation") whereas to read the Princeton transcript is to see that the emphasis is not on self-aggrandizement but conversely on how the self, like a bee, can learn to draw beauty from nature.

Although the discrepancies between the two passages seem

a unique, if bizarre, example of what can be discerned on the basis of different renditions of ostensibly the same evidence, in fact they call important attention to the ordinary case in which we receive different impressions when one rather than another quotation "represents" a text. The selection of quotations *creates* the case ostensibly being supported.[8] Crucial questions of interpretation therefore depend upon how the *Journal* text is to be excerpted. For example, will one talk about passages separated by a twenty-year gap as if they had sustained a continuity of thought? Alternatively, if one chooses to focus on a shorter period of time, on what basis will one decide that just these years are important? Assuming that one confines the discussion to a circumscribed period, why will not the very focus that legitimates inferences about related statements not preclude (and for the same reason) inferences about the whole enterprise? For any given entry, how will one decide where to begin and end a quotation, or on what aspect of a quotation to concentrate?

The problems to which I point apply to quotation of any literary text—to quotation of any text at all—but the *Journal*'s quite specific features make the ordinary liabilities of excerption seem to preclude its proper representation. Thus the inevitable distortion that accompanies quotation from any journal discourse is a consequence of the lack of narrative coherence, of inattention to—the presumptive absence of—an audience's expectations, hence of the arbitrariness of any passage on which the reader of such a journal might subsequently choose to focus. Quotation from Thoreau's *Journal* is further rendered suspect by Thoreau's aggressive attempt to disorganize the categories and conventions by which we customarily conceive of natural phenomena. In chapter five I elaborate the forms this impulse to disorganization takes.

Suffice it to say here that because Thoreau calls into question how natural phenomena are to be named, conceptualized and delimited by boundaries, he also implicitly makes problematic our procedures for identifying the quotations that are to represent these subjects. Where, for example, in any given case, are we to begin and end a quotation when the work's most pervasive critique derides the stability of such demarcations?

The act of thinking, Thoreau would maintain, specifically the act of thinking about nature, requires tolerating the very confusions and contradictions the *Journal*—in explicit terms—sees itself as replicating. In this way, Thoreau's *Journal,* which attempts to see the composition of nature, also attempts to make nature into a composition that will itself be faithful to natural elements. As I suggest in my concluding pages, we may familiarize these volumes—may, for example, discriminate the subjects which dominate one volume from those which dominate another, but such organizational acts by which we make sense of literary texts violate the forms of disorder the *Journal*'s discourse works to preserve. Thus a critic cannot be relied upon to provide representative portions of the work because, as I shall demonstrate, what would count as representative remains— and refuses—to be specified.

In this context it is interesting to consider the numerous anthologies of the *Journal* as extended acts of quotation, predicating "representative" passages on quite different criteria: passages isolated on the basis of their literary merit (Charles Anderson's *Thoreau's World,* 1971); "brief essays . . . which exemplify pieces of nature writing" (Walter Harding's *In the Woods and Fields of Concord: Selections from the Journals of Henry David Thoreau,* 1982); fragmentary but significant passages on nature supplemented by photographs (Herbert W. Gleason's *Through the Year With Thoreau,* 1917); passages "memorable" either "for their thought, for their beauty, or for their revelation of the man who wrote them and the times in which he lived" (Odell Shepard's *The Heart of Thoreau's Journals,* 1927); selections based on seasonal differences (H. G. O. Blake's *Early Spring in Massachusetts; Summer; Winter; Autumn,* 1881–1892); thematized subjects as implied by chapter headings like "Simply Seeing," "Walking By Night," "Standing at a Distance" (Laurence Stapleton's *H. D. Thoreau: A Writer's Journal,* 1960);[9] passages which conjoin entries from the *Journal* with Thoreau's other writings so as to exemplify attitudes about a particular natural phenomenon (William Howarth's *Thoreau in the Mountains: Writings by Henry David Thoreau,* 1982).

Quotation presents problems for the *Journal*'s critic in addition to the ones on which I have already remarked. It does so because, as the *Journal* is a text which most people have not seen, readers are more than customarily at the mercy of the unspecified biases of a critic who purports to be in possession of the literary goods; secondly, because Thoreau's own methods of quotation from the *Journal* (the passages he excerpts for the work he published) are not, as I shall explain below, necessarily the ones at which the *Journal*'s critic may want to look; primarily, however, because, as we have noted, even as Thoreau excerpts passages from his *Journal*, he simultaneously raises questions about any act of quotation that severs a part from a work he considers its own entity. In the different ways I have enumerated, the work seems to resist the representation that it simultaneously requires.

In my own pages quotation is not exempt from the distortions and difficulties I have enumerated. There is no way it could be. The point requires emphasis. My procedures for quotation and my discussion of quotation, especially in the fifth chapter, are meant to underline the insolubility of the difficulties I have exposed—to show in what ways passages from Thoreau's *Journal* are not hospitable to the excerption that we associate with the representation of literary texts. I nonetheless wish to specify the suppositions which dictate my choice of quotations and which are inseparable from such choice. (1) I shall contend in the following pages that the *Journal* is not (only) draft material for the writings Thoreau himself published, but that *Walden* and the *Journal* are autonomous writings; I shall, moreover, argue that *Walden* and the *Journal* are not just complementary, but make competitive claims and establish competitive alliances. (2) If the works are to be considered hierarchically, it may be the *Journal* which Thoreau understood to be the primary work, for it is *Walden* which is splintered from the *Journal*, not the other way around.[10] (3) If we accept the notion that Thoreau conceived of the *Journal* as his major work, we will need to reconsider what it means for an author to designate the work he kept "private" to be his principal work—a work intended to take precedence over what he himself published; such a case, reversing our ordinary suppositions, suggests an opposite relation between what is presentable and published, and, conversely, what is unpublished, unpresentable and *consequently* primary. If Thoreau did intend his *Journal* for publication (intended or not, within one year of Thoreau's death, it was being excavated for this purpose), the *Journal*'s "privacy" would be one of its most outrageous fictions, an idea whose exigencies I explore in my fourth chapter. (4) Given the options—that Thoreau intended a posthumous audience for the work or, alternatively, that for twenty-four years he wrote a book to which he alluded as "A Book of the seasons" (June 11, 1851 [5:477]) and which he fervently hoped no one would read—on a number of counts, the former is more attractive. For one thing, we have literary models for the first situation I am describing—Wordsworth's *Prelude*, for example, or Dickinson's poems.[11] For another, the first situation presents us with a less deranged picture of the man who wrote the work we are examining, for it interprets the *Journal*'s banishing of other men—a phenomenon I discuss in the fourth chapter—not as a psychological aberration but as a requisite condition of a literary experiment.

I wish to comment further about the relation between *Walden* and the *Journal* as I have described it above. For we continue to wonder about the indeterminate relation between the two texts. What happens when an editor becomes an author composing a second text by excerpting material from the first text on which—this is crucial—he continues to work? However speculative the answer, it is necessary to hazard one, and I do so as follows. The various revisions which culminate in *Walden* illustrate Thoreau's struggle to "represent" nature in the social forms that are receptive to it—the form of the essay, the homily, the didactic instruction. As the argument in the following pages implies, the transformation of material from *Journal* text to publishable text is not primarily stylistic. Rather, the transformation civilizes the features of the *Journal* text I shall proceed to discuss. This civilizing has consequences. Much has been written about Thoreau's aversion to the social world as it is recorded most emphatically in the first half of *Walden.* I do not, however, think it is the corruption of the social world per se that occasions Thoreau's ire. Rather, I think that Thoreau's impatience with, and grief over, society are largely a consequence of the concessions required by the *writing* of *Walden*. These concessions are exacting. They also are not easy. It takes seven drafts to cultivate nature, to formalize what Thoreau sees so that others can follow it. What is being "revised," then, is not primarily the text, but rather a passion for nature divorced from social meaning.

Near the end of *Walden* Thoreau worries out loud, "I fear chiefly lest my expression may not be *extra- vagant* enough, may not wander far enough beyond the narrow limits of my daily experience, so as to be adequate to the truth of which I have been convinced." "Extra vagance!" he muses; "it depends on how you are yarded."[12] In *Walden* Thoreau's speech is yarded of necessity. He must present his reverence for nature in a way that makes it accessible to others within the circumscriptions of literary conventions: by beginnings and endings and representative symbols. Moreover, he must show us that a life in nature is a life with a purpose. On the second page he tells us, "I would fain say . . . something about your condition, especially your outward condition or circumstances in this world, in this town, what it is, whether it is necessary that it be as bad as it is, whether it cannot be improved as well as not." The idea that watching nature is efficacious may just be a lure for what Thoreau really wants to tell us—that we ought to watch nature for the moral or the beauty of it—but the promise of nature's usefulness continues throughout *Walden*, which insists that to live in nature is to reap its rewards. Such enticement of an audience, such accommodation to an audience, inevitably changes Thoreau's perspective on his subject in *Walden*. To lessen the distance between the social and the natural, Thoreau must lessen—must coerce us into disbelieving in—the distance between the natural and the human. One adjustment requires the other. In the concessions by which *Walden* is yarded—by which it makes nature available to an audience—*Walden* presents not nature but the seductive rapprochement of the natural and the social to which, put in the harshest terms, nature is sacrificed. In the passage about speaking extravagantly to which I earlier alluded, Thoreau had added, "I desire to speak somewhere *without* bounds." Perhaps more than one would like, the *Journal* satisfies that desire.

The suppositions enumerated above dictate my discussion and choice of the passages that follow. Conventionally expressed: the passages dictate the suppositions. These alternative descriptions are not in fact exclusive. Although quotations range from the *Journal's* beginning to its end, I rely heavily on passages from the years 1850 to 1852, for I would maintain that it is during this time that Thoreau begins to regard—and to speak of—the *Journal* as an autonomous composition. It is also during this period that he speculates about a man's relation to nature and a man's relation to an audience, as these issues are crucial to the *Journal's* independent status. Moreover, during the two years in question, even by the most diverse standards of evaluation, the *Journal's* features change. It is therefore no coincidence that most "anthologies" of the *Journal* begin around these years or draw heavily upon them. Thus, as I have noted, by May 1850, entries become less sporadic. By December of 1850, they occur at several days' remove. By June of 1851, Thoreau is making daily records—a practice he continues until a few months before his death. It is interesting to remember what else is occurring during that two-year period.

By 1849, Thoreau had completed the first three versions of *Walden*. Between 1849 and late 1851 or early 1852, although Thoreau tinkered with *Walden*, adding quotations from Chinese and Hindu writings to it, as J. Lyndon Shanley tells us, he left it substantially alone.[13] After 1852 (again according to Shanley) he added up to sixty pages from the *Journal* years 1850–1852, most of it to chapters like "The Pond in Winter," "Spring," and "Sounds."[14] About the two-year distraction from the writing of *Walden* I have two observations: (1) that Thoreau did not convert the material of 1850–1852 from the *Journal* to *Walden* at the time of its composition because at that time he was not considering the former a draft but rather was regarding it as a primary composition, and (2) that when in 1852 he did begin to cannibalize this material for the latter part of *Walden* (which is, as we recall, the portion of the book which exposes man's relation to nature undistracted by the social world) he possessed knowledge of such a connection only because he had first learned in isolation—in the confines of the *Journal*—what he could never have learned in a work that had to answer to others (specifically the others of an "audience") about man's genuinely solitary relation to nature.[15] I would argue that the *Journal* text for the years 1850–1852 is not trial for a text which is later perfected. Rather, the perfection of Thoreau's knowledge, as *Walden* is its beneficiary, is itself a consequence of the primacy of the *Journal* composition which examines the experiment of a man living in solitude with nature, designating the record of that experience as closed to others' scrutiny.

Between 1850 and 1852 Thoreau exhibits a marked self-consciousness about the purpose of his enterprise, echoing, from an entirely different point of view, one of our questions: what kind of work is this? Thoreau's concern for the nature of his enterprise is revealed in several ways. It is revealed in his observations about the absence of literary precedents. On February 9, 1851: "It is remarkable how few passages comparatively speaking there are in the best literature of the day which betray any intimacy with nature" (5:352). Broadening the observation a few pages later in the same *Journal* entry: "I do not know where to find in any literature whether ancient or modern—an adequate [ac]count of that Nature with which I am acquainted. Mythology comes nearest to it of any" (5:354). On July 18, 1852: "I perceive that this, the natural side, has not got into literature" (IV:236). And of January 8, 1851: "I cannot think of any poetry which adequately expresses this yearning for the wild. the *wilde.*" (5:342). It is revealed in his rumination about choosing a vocation: "I feel myself uncommonly prepared for *some* literary work, but I can select no work" (September 7, 1851 [7:78–79]). On August 19, 1851, in his response to that dilemma: "What if a man were earnestly & wisely to set about recollecting & preserving the thoughts which he has had! How many perchance are now irrecoverable!" (6:705). Thoreau's concern about the status of the enterprise is revealed indirectly in his relation to an audience, for the *Journal* seems single-mindedly to be redefining not only the idea of a vocation or the function of journal writing, but the following contingent questions: How am I to understand my subject (my relation to nature) when it is unmediated by a social context? If I were truly separate from mankind, and could consider nature in isolation, to whom would I be speaking?

2

The Language of the Journal

How ample & generous was nature— My inheritance is not narrow—
Here is no other this evening . . . as if I . . . by my edicts excluded
men from my territories. . . . I walk as one . . . turned loose into the
woods the only man in nature. . . . (August 31, 1851 [7:38–39])

In the chapter "Solitude" in *Walden*, Thoreau asks a central
question: "What sort of space is that which separates a man
from his fellows and makes him solitary?" (*W*, 133). But the
question, which is a real one, is derailed by a declaration ("I
love to be alone")[16] and is rerouted first by a justification ("I
never found the companion that was so companionable as
solitude") and then by a series of analogic evasions: "The
sun is alone, except in thick weather. . . . God is alone,—but
the devil, he is far from alone . . . I am no more lonely than
a single mullein or dandelion in a pasture, or a bean leaf, or
sorrel, or a horse-fly, or a humble-bee. I am no more lonely
than the Mill Brook, or a weathercock, or the northstar, or
the south wind, or an April shower, or a January thaw, or
the first spider in a new house" (*W*, 137). If we return to the
intitial question, "What sort of space is that which separates
a man from his fellows and makes him solitary?" we see that
it contains overlapping considerations: why is there space
which makes men separate from each other? And: what are
the isolating manifestations of this condition? But the question also asks: What is *between* men? What do they have in
common despite, or as a consequence of, their separation?
Probings first after cause, then after the characteristics of the
mediating territory, give way in the discussion, however, to
a wholly different aspect of the question—one that turns

away from proximity and solicits alienation. Thoreau dismisses the reconciliatory connotations of his own question in order to make it mean, "What is it that makes me not even wish to consider my relations to others, but instead to be solitary?"

Not until the next chapter, "Visitors," do we see violence in the repudiation of community. So oppressed by that state of "intimate society" where we can "feel each other's breath" and where "animal heat and moisture" have no chance to evaporate, Thoreau there recalls his company pressing the chairs up against the walls in an effort to put adequate distance between one another, and even then, though the chairs were shoved apart "till they touched the wall in opposite corners . . . commonly there was not room enough" (W, 141). It is clear from the context of the passage from "Visitors" that such distance permits men not only to endure each other's company, but thereby best to profit from it: "As the conversation began to assume a loftier tone, we gradually shoved our chairs apart . . . ," etc. The idea of distance's enabling best contact, however, made especially cogent by the violence of the image of the chairs shoved apart, calls into question the enjoyment Thoreau claims he is validating. So the brutality of the image in that chapter's first sentence ("I think I love society as much as most, and I am ready enough to fasten like a blood-sucker for the time to any full-blooded man that comes in my way"), to my mind, repudiates the love of society it is ostensibly espousing.

In *Walden*, the question "What sort of space is that which separates a man from his fellows?" thus comes to mean "What are the reasons I want to eschew him?" The conversion of the question not only contradicts our sense of the proper relation of men to each other, but also fails to do justice to the complexity of Thoreau's deliberations about when he can entertain them without being distracted by the presence of society. In a passage of his *Journal*, Thoreau explains why the presence of others should be a distraction:

If I am too cold for human friendship—I trust I shall not soon be too cold for natural influences. It appears to be a law that you cannot have a deep sympathy with both man & nature. Those qualities which bring you near to the one estrange you from the other. (April 11, 1852 [10:680])[17]

Ktaadn and *A Week on the Concord and Merrimack Rivers* are books that repress despair at the idea of the incompatibility of the social and the natural by assigning men incidental roles, roles that, not crucial, can never collide with the central role of nature. In *Ktaadn*, as in *A Week*, people are bystanders; or, still nothing in their own right, their presence facilitates recuperation, as do landscapes in some fiction (I am thinking of the moment when Thoreau stumbles out of his transport at the suddenly apprehended awfulness of nature into the welcome company of fellow hikers). If *Walden* is that book which tries to achieve deep sympathy with man and with nature, to retrieve what Thoreau has learned in isolation and to socialize it for us, it tells two finally incompatible stories—of rapture at the natural world, of rage at the social one. Insofar as critics like Stanley Cavell have attended to the former, they conceive of *Walden* as a prophetic book whose grace lies in the fact that it can talk to and for us. Insofar as critics like Richard Bridgman have attended to the latter, they conceive of *Walden* as a book whose author needs rescue from his own despair. Each implicitly denies the way in which *Walden* suffers diversion from its own best subject: Thoreau's unmediated relation to nature.

Alfred Kazin implies a comparable idea when he insists that, contrary to popular belief, Thoreau was not too little in touch with his fellow men but rather "that the great fault of his writing and indeed the pathos of his life is that he was all too aware of what other men would think of him." Though he does not explain it, Kazin then draws an astonishing conclusion: "Had he not been so, he would never have written *Walden*."[18] In the following pages, I shall explore the meaning of such an apparently perverse assertion, for while my subject is not *Walden*—it is Thoreau's *Journal*—insofar as the two enterprises are goaded by antithetical aspirations, the examination of one throws light on the other. *Walden* and the *Journal* both purport to offer us "some such account as [a man] would send to his kindred from a distant land" (W, 1), the reading of which would enable "us to look through each other's eyes for an instant" (*W*, 10). The previous passage from *Walden* has its counterpart in the *Journal* in which, on July 16, 1851, Thoreau specifies "I speak as a witness on the stand and tell what I have perceived . . . I wondered if a mortal had ever known what I knew" (6:571). In the passage from *Walden*, the hyperbole of the rhetoric (the report sent from afar, the visionary look through the eyes of another) rests on the claim, however unarticulated, that at least for this man the story being told, not one in a repertoire, is, rather, unique. It is the case with respect to certain kinds of narratives—testaments, for example (and *Walden*, like the *Journal*, purports to be such a testament)—that they capture our attention just to the degree that their authors assert a singularity of vision. In practical terms, this means that, whatever the subject, we do not suppose we are being told one of many possible stories the man has at his command, but rather that this is the one story the man has to deliver. Hence the prophetic mode and the urgency of discourse. For the implication of a testament is that only this man can tell this story, and, concomitantly, that it is the one story this man can tell.

The premise of the following pages, however, is that the visions we see in *Walden* and the *Journal* diverge from each other, not because the two are hybrid compositions—one draft material for a primary other—but contrarily, because the experience of nature in *Walden* and the experience of nature in the *Journal* are incompatible. To appropriate Emerson's words and to transpose the context, the respective stories "do not believe in each other." *Walden* would produce an account of nature visible for others. The *Journal* turns its back on others in order to maintain: "There is no interpreter between us and our consciousness" (January 5, 1850 [2:84]). Which of these enterprises (and its assumptions) betrays the other? Which is the real work? Although the latter question is naive (for how we would answer such a question depends upon the criteria of assessment) it is less easy to dismiss the problematic conjunction of authenticity and exclusivity as it is alternatively presumed by *Walden* and the *Journal*. The two accounts proceeding in disregard of each other (*Walden* written over seven years and addressed to an immediate audience; the *Journal* written over

twenty-four years of oblivion to others) make such deliberations inevitable, forcing us to consider: what does it mean to
make an account of nature? To oneself? To others? What does
it mean to make concessions that would translate private into
public? What is the cost of refusing these concessions? I shall
elaborate on these questions. At the moment I wish to turn
directly, however, to Thoreau's *Journal,* in which nature is *a
priori* dominant. Nor does the *Journal* convert the human into a
background, as do *Ktaadn* or *A Week,* for the *Journal's* premise is
that Thoreau has freed himself from the obligatory engagement
with the human which would instigate dialectical terms such as
"background" and "foreground." The natural and the human
are, in fact, locked in opposition, but the opposition is daring
to the precise degree that the very idea of a conflict appears to
have been settled. Thus the *Journal* reinstates the question,
"What sort of space is that which separates a man from his
fellows and makes him solitary?" while not, as *Walden* does,
permitting its evasion.

In *Walden* the pond is looked at and personified: "Walden, is
it you?" Thoreau asks, gazing at the reflection in the water and
recognizing it as if human. Thoreau may be concerned that
nature is a "stranger," but individual descriptions cultivate the
strangeness. In personifications, Thoreau alternatively writes
about the body of the pond; about the pond as the "earth's
eye," and of the color of its iris; about the pond as a face
uncreased by the water's ripples; about the shore as the pond's
lips. Conversely, the self recognizes its image in nature, asking: "Am I not partly leaves and vegetable mould myself?" The
beauty of *Walden* is the ease with which its speaker presumes
such connections. In the *Journal* identifications between nature
and human nature are less frequent, though in the following
passages, we see how they are accomplished. Nature is internalized and the body externalized through tropes of inversion:

I hear the sound of Heywood['s] Brook falling into Fair Haven Pond—
inexpressibly refreshing to my senses—it seems to flow through my
very bones.— I hear it with insatiable thirst— It allays some sandy
heat in me— It affects my circulations—methinks my arteries have

sympathy with it What is it I hear but the pure water falls within me, in the circulation of my blood—the streams that fall into my heart? (July 11, 1851 [6:562])

If the previous figure shows us how the self internalizes aspects of nature, the following figure shows us how nature externalizes aspects of the self:

The earth I tread on is not a dead inert mass. It is a body—has a spirit is organic—and fluid to the influence of its spirit. . . . To be sure it is somewhat foecal and stercoral—. So the poet's creative moment is when the frost is coming out in the spring—but as in the case of some too easy poets—if the weather is too warm & rainy or long continued it becomes mere diarrhea—mud & clay relaxed. The poet must not have something pass his bowels merely—that is women's poetry.— He must have something pass his brain & heart and bowels too, it may be, altogether.—so he gets delivered— There is no end to the fine bowels here exhibited—heaps of liver—lights & bowels. Have you no bowels? Nature has some bowels. and there again she is mother of humanity. Concord is a worthier place to live in—the globe is a worthier place for these creations This slumbering life—that may wake. Even the solid globe is permeated by the living law. It is the most living of creatures. (December 31, 1851 [8:356–357])

The passage in which Heywood's Brook is converted to "the circulation of my blood—the streams that fall into my heart" and the passage in which the "solid globe" is bequeathed "bowels" and a body enact familiar transformations. Through similar tropes in *Walden* we are shown how, in spring, the earth sloughs itself off. The tropes are familiar not simply because we have seen them—or ones like them—before. They are familiar because they do not get us to see anything alien. Rendering the alien has actually domesticated it. In addition, although the power of each equation depends upon its proposing an analogy which is then worked out, the equative self-sufficiency is also a limitation. Once the waterfall is resituated in the heart, and the bowels are seen to issue from the earth, we are implicitly asked not to think further about the meaning of the relocations. To think further would undo resolutions which depend upon following the stages, and recognizing the terminus, of linguistic connections which rest their case on seeing relationship as equivalence.

In other passages of the *Journal*, however, Thoreau insists on the lack of consonance between the natural and the human. On July 19, 1851, he writes: "Methinks my seasons revolve more slowly than those of nature, I am differently timed" (6:584). Eight months later the observation is more critical: "Though the frost is nearly out of the ground the winter has not broken up in me. It is a backward season with me. Perhaps we grow older & older till we no longer sympathize with the revolution of the seasons—& our winters never break up" (March 30, 1852 [10:634]). On March 31, 1852, he muses on the difference between human and other creatures: "I see that the sparrow cheeps & flits & sings adequately to the great design of the universe—that man does not communicate with it,— understand its language because he is not at one with nature" (10:640). Casting the distinction in terms neither chronological nor generic but rather in a morally contrastive context: "It would be worth the while to tell why a swamp pleases us.— what kinds please us. . . . Why the moaning of the storm gives me pleasure. Methinks it is because it puts to rout the trivialness of our fairweather life & gives it at least a tragic interest. . . . There is something worth living for when we are resisted—threatened" (March 31, 1852 [10:638–639]). In many passages of the *Journal* the reconciliation of nature and human nature is less sanguinely problematic:

What is this beauty in the Landscape but a certain fertility in me? I look in vain to see it realized but in my own life. If I could wholly cease to be ashamed of myself—I think that all my days would be fair. (October 31, 1850 [4:238])

Although the first sentence equates nature and the self ("What is this beauty in the landscape but a certain fertility in me?"), in the second we are told that the two are incommensurate ("I look in vain to see it realized but in my own life"). The hyperbole in the first sentence instigates the critique of the second. Yet here, as in other entries of the *Journal*, something appears to be missing. What is missing is the acknowledgment that the relation between the two sentences is one of contradiction rather than of development. The telling of a double story—in the case of the previous passage the story of continuity suggested by the consecutive sentences/the story of revision suggested by the contradictory content of the two sentences—is characteristic of the *Journal*'s figuration. Doubleness manifests itself differently in the following passage, where the narrative does not reverse its assertions but rather questions their meaning:

if I could so live that there should be no desultory moment in all my life! That in the trivial season when small fruits are ripe my fruits might be ripe also that I could watch nature always with my moods! (August 17, 1851 [6:686])

Even if we understand "the trivial season" of nature to imply those insignificances of nature which demand attention, the explanation is problematic. To seek to harness one's attention to trivialities complicates the imperative that the mind must not wander, because it inadvertently explains why the mind is wandering (what it would have to fix on, could it train itself to constancy, would only be trivialities) rather than to provide reasons which compel the mind's attention. Further vexing the clarity of the passage, the state which is desired—the state in which I am to watch nature with my moods—implies a capriciousness of response akin to the word "desultory" to which we would have thought an alternative was being posed. For although what is implored is a perpetual fitness or fittedness, rather than skittishness, the idea of moods introduces, if only in passing, the second connotation. Thus the description of the constancy solicited calls its fact into question. In conjunction with these two complications (describing the imperative for attention in words that rather explain the deflection of attention; advocating constancy of attention by reference to states of mind defined by inconstancy) the formulation raises additional questions. The idea that the self can know nature not by abandoning the self but by adhering to it suggests that access and emotion accompany each other. Emotion *is* access, and in Thoreau's formulation it stands between nature and the self as that which simultaneously differentiates the two (the self has an

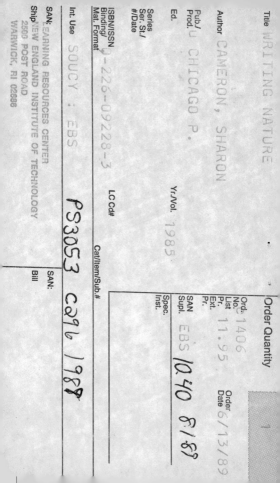

identity separate from what it feels, as nature has an identity separate from what is felt about it) and brings the two together (the self absorbed by its moods subordinates its whole history to the sway of a dominant moment, as the world is absorbed by the drift of a particular feeling in the contours of which, time and again, it takes fundamental shape).

But if the fluctuations of nature are akin to the fluctuations of moods, would watching nature be the same thing as watching one's moods? Then what is being implied about how attention to oneself will create attention to nature, especially as what shifts in one case are the features of nature and what shifts in the other are the states of mind that are to register it? Finally, does the proposition imply that one is separate from one's moods—that one runs the danger of standing outside of them? If the first passage suggests that man cannot be one with nature, the second suggests he may also not properly be able to experience it. The confidence of the second assertion is subverted by the implication that, though defined by our moods, we may also be oblivious to them, may stand not simply outside nature, but outside our own natures. Then the question of seeing properly poses a prior question of proper being. The two passages read together propose a series of implicit questions: Is the life in me commensurate with the life in nature? If not, how can I see what I am unable to become? And more baffling still, how do I understand a relationship determined by something between nature and myself—not in the circumscribed territory of either?

It is the latter question—which seeks to know the terms of mediation between the self and nature—that occupies a major portion of the *Journal*. The mediation is unstable because the entities brought together—nature and the self—are perpetually redefined, and with respect to themselves as well as to each other:

When I have been confined to my chamber for the greater part of several days by some employment or perchance by the ague—till I felt weary & house-worn—I have been conscious of a certain softness to which I am otherwise & commonly a stranger—in which the gates were loosened to some emotions— And if I were to become a con-

firmed invalid I see how some sympathy with mankind & society
might spring up
    Yet what is my softness good for even to tears— It is not I but
nature in me. (November 11, 1851 [8:273])

"It is not I but nature," the speaker claims, disassociating himself from sympathy. But the repudiation is complicated because
the prepositional phrase "nature in me" acknowledges that
sympathy issues from the self, and therefore is internal to it.
Maybe what is being suggested is that how the self defines itself
is not dependent upon complete association with the impulses
that inhabit it, but rather that the self can be defined in defiance
of those impulses, at least of their totality. Definition does not
specify that all that is interior is integral to the self, nor that all
that is exterior is alien to the self. It predicates a different notion
of identity, contigent not upon bodily inclusion or exclusion, but
rather upon that confluence of impulses and experiences imagined ideally to be one. The confluence of impulses has nothing
to do with actual experience, nor with total experience, nor with
inner experience. And as interiority or actuality fails to identify
the self, so the attribution of sympathy to (one's own) nature is a
statement about the origin of sympathy, not about its essence,
about where it comes from, not what it is. In fact to specify that
sympathy arises from human nature separates it from myself.
This way of putting it suggests that between myself and my
nature there is a disjunction.
    I have asserted that the passage does not incline us to asso-
ciate nature with the body where a connection would involve
simple internalization (waterfalls in the heart) or simple externalization (bowels issuing from the earth). It forbids the equation by insisting that the body and the self, nature and my
nature, far from being identical, are antagonistic. The passage
does not then simplify the idea of antagonism. It suggests that
the foreign and the familiar are not static entities (as the self,
for example, is not a static entity) but are subject to change.
Moreover, the disavowal of tenderness ("what is my softness
good for. . . .") bears a subtle connection to its still existing
fact, for the tenderness questioned is reiterated in the question.
The impulse for tears and the exasperation at that impulse

accompany each other. As a consequence, the observation discourages as illegitimate any fast distinction between nature and human nature, for these two terms (like the foreign and the familiar, the internal and the external, sympathy and its disclaimer) are suddenly not separable, and for the same reasons. The nature to which Thoreau refers is human nature. But because human nature is a force in the self over which it has no control, it is kin to that larger force from whose unruliness Thoreau chooses not to distinguish it.

I suggested in chapter one that phenomena in Thoreau's *Journal* were isolated from each other as if to create a clear space for vision. But vision for what? What is being viewed? In some of the passages at which I have looked nothing is being viewed; things are rather being transformed, as in the internalization of the landscape or the externalization of the body. But if we presume that nature is being viewed and with the self's moods—in the transformation of those moods, in all their incompleteness (Emerson had cautioned: "We must hold hard to this poverty, however scandalous")—then we will see that Thoreau questions the connection between objects in the landscape and the self who regards them. As in the meditation previously examined, what Thoreau poses are essentially philosophical questions about nature and the self, specifically, as the passages to which I turn now indicate, about the relation between nature and the mind:

> Is there such virtue in raking cranberries—that those men's industry whom I now see on the meadow—shall reprove my idleness? Can I not go over those same meadows after them & rake still more valuable fruits. Can I not rake with my mind? Can I not rake a thought perchance which shall be worth a bushel of cranberries? (September 7, 1851 [7:91])

The repetitive questions themselves seem to rake the subject under consideration, to go over and over it. What is being rehearsed or gone over? It is not, as it might be, whether virtue inheres in industry or idleness. The passage rather turns its attention to the status of an act in the mind, and it presumes—at least initially—that the raking of the mind and the raking of cranberries occur on the same ground. We will want to know what sense it makes to say such a thing. Emerson, in *Nature*, had insisted on a certain sublimity arising from the fact that "while the world is a spectacle, something in man is stable." Not for Thoreau, whose successive visions of nature first record their own place of origin, and are then superimposed upon each other until the idea of a view—that which is seen, and the perspective from which it is seen—are thoroughly confused. In this case what is confused is the status of objects and their relation to thoughts. While it initially seems a distinction is being made (between raking and idleness, between raking and thinking), as it turns out, a comparison is being made between the two activities. If thinking and raking do overlap, it is not, as we might suppose, because they are the same kind of activity— each, for example, arduous. The claim for their coincidence is rather that both occur "over those same meadows"; that is, in the same place. Further discomposing the stability of the connection is the fact that while in one sentence we are told thinking *is* raking, a sentence later we are told *thought* is being raked. Thus the parts of the analogy (thinking to raking/cranberries to thought) are not commensurate, for what is unearthed by thought is an integral part of itself.

Yet maybe the passage does not mean to brag about what thought can do. Maybe it means to acknowledge what thought cannot do. Such an acknowledgment could be discerned in the adjustment of terms—in the fact that the criterion for the comparison of thinking and raking (the externality of both) gives way to another criterion of comparison (one not predicated on externality, but rather predicated on value): "Can I not rake a thought perchance which shall be worth a bushel of cranberries?" Then grounds for comparison would shift to questions about value. Yet the question of value, like the question of place, is inhospitable to the comparison of things as dissimilar as cranberries and thoughts. Nor is it conceivable that one same assessment could say anything intelligible about the these two phenomena. But Thoreau half wishes to hold on to the idea he has apparently relinquished—the idea that thought can be like an object, that thought can be an object. Another way to say this is to suggest that Thoreau wants to discover the depth of thought not inside himself but inside nature. He wants its externality legitimated. This is different from wanting to get the body out of itself, onto the earth, which involves externalizing something already palpable. Here the point of the externalization is to *confer* palpability, not to reposition it. Thoreau wants thinking to be about something other than itself, to be something other than it is. In the following passages we are told what it would look like were it so redefined:

> In proportion as I have celestial thoughts is the necessity for me to be out and behold the western sky before sunset these winter days. That is the symbol of the unclouded mind that knows neither winter nor summer. What is your thought like? That is the hue—that the purity & transparency and distance from earthly taint of my inmost mind—for whatever we see without is a symbol of something within—& that which is farthest off—is the symbol of what is deepest within. (January 17, 1852 [9:407])

The commonsense reading of the passage suggests that, through an inversion of the grammar, "inmost mind" and "earthly taint" keep "distance" from each other. But an opposite reading of the passage—one urged by the idea of liberating thought from the mind, of wishing to behold it as an externality—rather suggests the same grammar makes "mind" and "taint" bleed into each other, as if the mental had suddenly become material. Hence Thoreau seeks "distance from earthly taint of my inmost mind," seeks thought which, detached from the mind, is pure and transparent. The hue of "the unclouded mind" is like "the western sky before sunset" not only because inside and outside represent each other (this is suggested by the end of the passage), but also, and oppositely (this is suggested by the middle of the passage) because the western sky looks like thought free of the mind; it looks like nothing at all. In the effort to disassociate thought from any particular coloration, from the tint of materiality as well as from its taint (Thoreau implies the characteristics are integral), to see the unclouded mind that knows neither winter nor summer, it is as if Thoreau were asking: What would thought look like free from the taint of inmost mind? If it were externalized, then could I see it? If it had no object, would there be anything left for me to see? Underlying the ambiguities to which I have been pointing, the revelation of the passage lies just in the way the typological similitude, which reenacts the idea that phenomena in nature prefigure the self's essence, is disrupted by the question ("What is your thought like?") that it was meant to answer.

Elsewhere Thoreau turns his attention from the question of where thought is (inside or outside, in the mind or on the ground) and from the question of how it appears (as an object or a transparency), from the question of whether in lieu of having an object it has an appearance, to ask about thought's origin: "While I am abroad the ovipositors plant their seeds in me I am fly blown with thought—& go home to hatch—& brood over them" (July 23, 1851 [6:616]). What is born in reflection, at least in this reflection, is the germ of something external to the self. This way of putting it does not so much abolish the distinction made by the previous passage (between the ground of the field and the ground of the mind) as it shows us the moment of convergence during which the two legitimate each other. The emphasis of the passage is on the fact that thought has an object and origin outside the self—an idea reiterated literally in the next sentence, which insists that reflection turns the self back upon the world: "I was too discursive & rambling in my thought for the chamber & must go where the wind blows on me walking." Thoreau wants to be the externality on which he reflects, to be away from the self, to be out of the mind, and how thoroughly these desires spatialize themselves is apparent in the reflection "I seem to be more constantly merged in nature—my intellectual life is more obedient to nature than formerly. . . . O if I could be discontented with myself! If I could feel anguish at each descent!" (October 12, 1851 [8:219–220]). The self is the depth to which he doesn't want to sink. But this rupture from the self, precipitating as it does delivery to the outside world, is not always possible. It is sometimes prohibited because the very externality so ardently courted repels not simply merging but contact itself:

A cold & dark afternoon the sun being behind clouds in the west The landscape is barren of objects— the trees being leafless—& so little light in the sky for variety. Such a day as will almost oblige a man to eat his own heart. A day in which you must hold on to life by your teeth— You can hardly ruck up any skin on nature's bones— The sap is down—she wont peel. Now is the time to cut timber for yokes & ox bows—leaving the tough bark on—yokes for your own neck. Finding yourself yoked to matter & to Time. Truly a hard day. . . . Crickets gone into winter quarters— Friends long since gone there—& you left to walk on frozen ground—with your hands in your pockets. Ah but is not this a glorious time for your deep inward fires?— & will not your green hickory & white oak burn clear—in this frosty air? Now is not your manhood taxed by the great Assessor? Taxed for having a soul—a rateable soul. A day when you cannot pluck a flower—cannot dig a parsnip nor pull a turnip for the frozen ground—what do the thoughts find to live on? What avails you now the fire you stole from heaven? Does not each thought become a vulture to gnaw your vitals? . . .

Now there is nothing—not even the cold beauty of ice crystals—& snowy architecture. Nothing but the echo of your steps over the frozen ground (November 13, 1851 [8:279–280])

We are told the landscape is barren of objects, and bareness instigates a proliferation of images, as the speaker tries to get a hold on something outside himself. Yet the objects introduced for contemplation quickly give way, for conception is deprived of a surface outside the self to which it could adhere. The perilousness of holding onto life by the teeth is italicized by the thinness of what is being gripped ("You can hardly ruck up any skin on nature's bones"). Specifying the minimalness seems to exhaust the subject, which is quickly replaced by a succession of other thoughts similarly too sparse to be developed. The bleakness described prompts the idea of metaphoric consolation, "deep inward fires." The passage, though, remains faithful to the idea of separation. Man can neither get hold of the tree ("The sap is down—she wont peel") nor can he be the tree. He can make a trope of the latter, can describe himself as "green hickory & white oak" that will "burn clear." But this manner of speaking does not end the reflection; it rather acknowledges its own illegitimacy ("What avails you now the fire you stole from heaven?"). The moment Thoreau introduces the idea of inward fires is the moment he sees that a figure of speech sounds its own falseness. Man's soul and his thought can neither freeze nor burn the way matter does. The passage is filled with nostalgia for physical contact—holding onto life with one's teeth, being yoked to matter, plucking a flower, pulling a turnip from the ground. Such connections, although imagined, are not in fact palpable. There is no answer to the question "what do the thoughts find to live on?" One's very expression of despair dramatizes figures of speech—to eat your heart out, gnaw your vitals—not materializations, making metaphors of physicality where physicality does not exist.

I have shown that Thoreau wants thought out of the mind and on solid ground. He has also wished to see the externality, to witness the unclouded mind in the hue of the sky. In yet another passage he dramatizes a pun on conception. Though born in the mind, thought comes from the outside from a seed of nature. In each of the passages it initially seems that thought is being viewed. A cumulative look suggests rather that the point of the externalization is not thought's visibility but rather its expression, for Thoreau appears to be demonstrating the way in which language is the externality which brings thought and nature together: "Only thought which is expressed by the mind in repose as it were lying on its back & contemplating the heavens—is adequately & fully expressed" (July 8, 1851 [5:546]). Here, as previously, Thoreau is in search of something like moods which will stand between nature and the mind connecting the two, making them continuous.

I wish, however, to emphasize the peculiarity of my observation. What is between the mind and the heavens is part of the mind. What mediates two separate phenomena is one of those phenomena "in complete view." Because it is difficult to separate mind from its own thought (we recall a similar redundancy in the passage that employed the mind in raking a thought), we do not know how to understand what a connection between mind and nature would legitimately mean, for no discrete term brings them together. The very continuity expression was to have created seems to have preceded it, seems presupposed by it. Alternatively put, the very continuity expression was to have created is preempted by the questionable status of an absent third term. We know that the conventional way of representing connection between two unlike entities is by figuration, by metaphor or analogy. But examining Thoreau's figures of speech we see a linguistic corollary to the confusion I have noted. Thus the following straightforward analogy between the human and the natural calls the status of the analogy—what it means and how it functions—into question:

The clouds are *white* watery not such as we had in the winter— I see in this fresh morning the shells left by the muskrats along the shore— & their galleries leading into the meadow—& the bright red cranberries washed up along the shore—in the old water-mark. Suddenly there is a blur on the placid surface of the waters—a rippling mistiness produced as it were by a slight morning breeze.— And I should be sorry to show it to the stranger now— So it is with our minds. (April 2, 1852 [10:651–652])

What is like the mind? The blurring of the placid surface? The fact that freshness changes? That lucidity is subject to transformations over which it has no control? What is like the mind? We retain the fact of relation long before we understand its meaning. When we do understand it, it seems that Thoreau's ability to make a precise observation takes a clear mind, a mind not broken up or blurred. The lucid comment itself denies, at least for the moment, the analogy that likens the pond's confusion to that of the mind. Conversely, the analogy if true is preempted in Thoreau's possessive assertion "I should be sorry to show it to a stranger now" (as if it were his to show), this assertion presupposing an already pre-established relation—one therefore that does not need to be made by figuration. On the one hand, the truth of the analogy is called into question. On the other hand, the gratuitousness of the analogy becomes clear when its truth is assumed. The link between the mind and the pond fails to exist, or oppositely conceived, it exists *a priori*. Connection is neither erased nor is it made by the analogic merger.

Having now examined a number of Thoreau's figurations, we are in a position to ask: "What is it we have examined? Thoreau's thoughts about nature? Or his investigations of thought?" My question is instigated by the repetitive insistence on the conjunction of the two: watching nature with my moods; raking with the mind; celestial thoughts compelling one to behold the western sky, to behold the symbol of the unclouded mind; ovipositers planting their seeds in the self so it is flyblown with thought; thought gnawing its own vitals in a winter freeze because it cannot get a hold on the outside world; the blurring of the pond's surface as it is equated with the blurring of the mind. The very quotations which suggest that what is being sought is knowledge of nature simultaneously suggest that what is being sought is knowledge of the mind. Hence Thoreau asks: "What do the thoughts find to live on?", "What is your thought like?" and he insists, "Only thought which is expressed by the mind . . . lying on its back & contemplating the heavens—is . . . fully expressed." Apparently to write about nature is to write about how the mind sees nature, and sometimes about how the mind sees itself.

Yet when the mind sees nature what it sees is its difference from nature, is the way in which correspondences fail to work out. The subversion of correspondence can take the form of indirect contradiction, as when the claim that beauty in the landscape is fertility in me is peremptorily refuted by a following sentence. Alternatively, connection can be subverted not by a contradiction between the content of two consecutive sentences but rather by ambiguity within a single sentence—like the imperative which compels the mind to attend to nature but which does so in language which rather explains why attention might be wandering. Or correspondence can be established in those explicit terms which call its meaning into question, as when the self is shown to be alien rather than equal to its own nature. Finally, in those instances in which Thoreau invokes figuration to mediate the discrepancy between the mind and outside nature, the tropes of mediation sabotage its fact either because the third term which would connect the mind to nature is illegitimate (it is not a third term but is part of the mind), or because that third term, and figuration itself, is gratuitous (the mind and the pond need not be connected; they are already presumed to be part of one another).[19]

The harmony and confluence so central to Thoreau's other works and to Emerson's *Nature* (with which Thoreau's *Journal* can profitably be compared), in which nature and the mind evoke each other, is posited by the *Journal* so as to be frustrated. Thoreau may endorse the proposition that words are signs of natural facts, but since you cannot rake a thought as you would rake a cranberry, such propositions have no corollaries in actual experience. To invoke this as an example may be to demonstrate an insufficient understanding of what a metaphor is, yet it is by obstreperously and, at times, incongruously, trying to work such metaphors out that Thoreau's figuration in the *Journal* proposes and subverts the idea of correspondence. The whole of nature may be a metaphor for the human mind, but Thoreau's formulations emphasize *failed* attempts to make sense of the congruence. Another way to put this is to say that while Emerson acknowledges separations (hence man is "disunited with himself," hence "the ruin or the blank we see when we look at nature, is in our own eyes") for Emerson correspondence and its absence are absolute states, not necessarily incompatible with each other, whereas in the *Journal*, Thoreau labors to show the way in which one turns into the other.

For an extended discussion of the differences between the two, one would want to look at Joel Porte's *Emerson and Thoreau*, which, suggesting that Thoreau's interest in nature is not goaded by the impulse to find moral correlatives between nature and the mind but is primarily experimental, offers a useful corrective to F. O. Matthiessen's notion, advanced in *American Renaissance*, that, albeit on a practical level, Thoreau's philosophy merely replicates Emerson's.[20] Yet caricatures of the two ideas have governed our thinking, falsely suggesting that if Thoreau is not a poor man's Emerson, he is, as it were, a man without a mind, though one with compensatory characteristics, namely a love of sensation. Stanley Cavell's *The Senses of Walden* would rescue Thoreau from these unhappy alternatives. But Cavell's repetitive allusions to other philosophic figures suggest, to my mind, that in its own right Thoreau's position escapes coherence. Why Thoreau courts comparisons is an interesting question. From the repeated critical impulses to understand Thoreau by looking away from his own work, one would have to acknowledge that something about his writing barricades itself against investigation. Thus I would argue that

Walden's philosophic position is difficult to get hold of precisely because it theatricalizes attitudes in which, from the vantage of the *Journal's* language, it appears Thoreau does not believe. In *Walden* we are often conscious of postures of credence. With only *Walden* before us, we can feel we have two options: to ask other writers to gloss what we are reading, or, alternatively, to see *Walden* as a book that is deeply evasive about the complexity of Thoreau's feelings—specifically evasive about the possibility of a reconciliation between the mind and nature. It is this evasiveness which enables Walter Benn Michaels to talk about the "false bottoms of *Walden.*"[21] My own discussion is hardly exempt from the comparative procedures to which I allude, though in the case of the *Journal* comparisons are differently necessitated.

In the *Journal* Thoreau turns his back on the relation between the social and the natural to explore the relation between the natural and the human—a relation inhospitable to the values and conventions of critical discourse, social by definition. To get at the *Journal*, then, is to do so indirectly (in my discussion, through *Walden*). The point of my readings of the previous passages, though, has not been to demonstrate the literary features of Thoreau's *Journal.* It has rather been to demonstrate the way in which literary features—specifically, analogic connections between the mind and the ground, the mind and the sky, the mind and the pond—are ostentatiously thwarted. This is opposite to the literary troping of, and the consequent claims made by, *Walden*. In the *Journal* analogies do not inaugurate connections between nature and the mind. They rather call attention to the impossibility of such connection. As a consequence, we would expect Thoreau's examination of nature to dead-end, to halt at the finding that figurative connections are fraudulent. As I shall show in the next chapter, however, the *Journal* surprises us by producing a new kind of discourse to which the failed analogies cede.

In the *Journal*, contact with nature, unmediated by the social world, allows Thoreau to see—and more to the point to say—the ways in which he is separate from the nature that he loves. Like all intimate relations, this one forces inconsolable recognitions. Thus in examining the self's connection to nature the

Journal risks more than *Walden* does, but in the end, I would argue, it concedes absolutely nothing. Contemplating the originality of the profession on which he is embarking, Thoreau sees that it is not to be accommodated by traditional means: "I feel myself uncommonly prepared for *some* literary work, but I can select no work" (Sept. 7, 1851 [7:78–79]). Elaborating, he announces that he wants to write sentences which lie "like boulders on the page":

Sentences which are expensive towards which so many volumes—so much life went—which lie like boulders on the page—up & down [or] across. Not mere repetition but creation. which contain the seed of other sentences. Which a man might sell his grounds & castle to build. (August 22, 1851 [7:14])

Lest we think the analogy has a literary emphasis, we are corrected: "A writer a man writing is the scribe of all nature—he is the corn & the grass & the atmosphere writing" (September 2, 1851 [7:44]). Thoreau can find no model for his work because he is constructing a model. It is insufficient to say that he wants to record nature or to take its dictation. He also wants to incarnate its articulating will, and he is concerned, moreover, with the preservation of his labor. On January 1, 1852, Thoreau puts it thus: "I wish to be translated to the future—& look at my work *as* it were at a structure on the plain, to observe what portions have crumbled under the influence of the elements" (8:364–365). The idea that Thoreau is writing nature or is nature writing itself accounts for the *Journal*'s radical generic strangeness, and it contributes to our sense of subversion of the human.

To understand the meaning of Thoreau's claims—that he is the atmosphere writing, that he is first replicating nature, and then actually creating it, and that the creation prohibits access (boulders across the page which make its meanings unavailable)—requires further examination. Specifically, it requires examination first of Thoreau's attempt to write about nature that is divorced from the mind's symbolizing procedures and, second, of the generic consequences implied by such linguistic self-abnegation—issues discussed, in that order, in the following two chapters. What I have tried to do preliminarily is to lay the groundwork for these considerations, to show that ideas about the self's relation to nature accompany and precipitate the redefinition of a literary enterprise. For once Thoreau sees that correspondences between nature and the self are incomplete and uncompletable, what he would like to do is to prohibit them entirely. So doing, he would preserve the idea that nature is alien. But my claim is a complex and an apparently contradictory one, for the way Thoreau imagines that nature is alien is by also imagining he could impersonate the alienness— that he could voice nature or be nature's voice. When Thoreau insists he wants to write sentences that "lie like boulders on the page" or to be "the corn & the grass & the atmosphere writing," he does not mean nature can express the human or be expressed by it—either of these claims would be conventionally indebted to metaphor or analogy. Rather he says he can abandon the human, can make himself into the alienness he was forced to confront.

3

Natural Relations

The best thought is not only without somberness—but without morality. The universe lies outspread in floods of white light to it. The
moral aspect of nature is a disease caught of man—a jaundice im-
ported into her—To the innocent there are no cherubims nor angels.
Occasionally we rise above the necessity of virtue into an unchange-
able morning light—in which we have not to choose in a dilemma
between right and wrong—but simply to live right on and breathe the
circumambient air. (August 1, 1841 [*Journal* 1:315])

I

I have suggested that notwithstanding the sequentiality of
entries in the *Journal*, Thoreau strives toward a randomness of
impressions. Perhaps this is because he seeks to represent the
fact that the stance from which we look envelops only one of
infinite perspectives. On March 29, 1852: "It is but a day or two
that I have seen a boat on the meadows. The water on them has
looked very dark from the street. Their color depends on the
position of the beholder in relation to the direction of the wind"
(10:630). The illusion that what we see could be anything but
relative is reiterated by the self who knows that its angle will
determine not simply perspective but the content of the vision:
"You sit twenty feet above the still river—see the sheeny pads.
& the moon & some bare tree tops in the distant horizon. Those
bare tree tops add greatly to the wildness" (September 7, 1851
[7:88]). However he may acknowledge that the beholder ar-
ranges the composition he sees, Thoreau in the *Journal* would
relinquish control as an organizing intelligence. "I begin to
see . . . objects only when I leave off understanding them," he
reports (February 14, 1851 [5:366]). On September 13, 1852:

"Carlyle said that how to observe was to look, but I say that it is rather to see, and the more you look the less you will observe" (IV:351). And: "I do not know that knowledge amounts to anything more definite than a novel & grand surprise [on] a sudden revelation of the insufficiency of all that we had called knowledge before" (February 27, 1851 [5:377]). The *Journal* is the record of a man who would abandon not simply human concerns but perceptual givens. Although Thoreau acknowledges the eye's determination, he conversely insists that seeing can be made to precede the impositions of meaning. I wish to explore the ramifications of this fiction, but I want first to comment on the ways it skews the implications of an otherwise conventional assertion: "You might say of a philosopher that he was in this world as a spectator" (October 31, 1850 [4:251]), for Thoreau's rejections of *a priori* meaning specifically prohibit conjunctions which we associate with the most elemental kind of thinking. What then does it mean to associate philosophy and seeing? In a statement I take to be inadvertently connected to the issues of randomness, of sight, of the avoidance of interpretation which we have been considering, Thoreau writes:

My Journal should be the record of my love. I would write in it only of the things I love. My affection for any aspect of the world. What I love to think of. I have no more distinctness or pointedness in my yearnings than an expanding bud—which does indeed point to flower & fruit to summer & autumn—but is aware of the warm sun & spring influence only. (November 16, 1851 [4:275–276])

Here love and aimlessness are wedded to each other, for "what I love to think of" has no intent. What the passage exemplifies most singularly is not so much affection, or the *Journal* as its document, as the source of the phenomenon that generates both. If the self can submit to the perfect pointlessness of experience it will be naturalized, and brought to fruition. Against the radical claim, "I have no more distinctness or pointedness in my yearnings than an expanding bud," *Walden* will tell us:

I went to the woods because I wished to live deliberately, to front only the essential facts of life, and see if I could not learn what it had to teach, and not, when I came to die, discover that I had not lived. I did not wish to live what was not life, living is so dear; nor did I wish to practise resignation, unless it was quite necessary. I wanted to live deep and suck out all the marrow of life, to live so sturdily and Spartan-like as to put to rout all that was not life, to cut a broad swath and shave close, to drive life into a corner, and reduce it to its lowest terms, and, if it proved to be mean, why then to get the whole and genuine meanness of it, and publish its meanness to the world; or if it were sublime, to know it by experience, and be able to give a true account of it in my next excursion. (W, 90–91)

The chapter, "Where I Lived, and What I Lived For," from which the paragraph comes, concludes its bid for our attention by the claim with which the book gifts us:

If you stand right fronting and face to face to a fact, you will see the sun glimmer on both its surfaces, as if it were a cimeter, and feel its sweet edge dividing you through the heart and marrow, and so you will happily conclude your mortal career. Be it life or death, we crave only reality. (W, 98)

Although the two passages seem opposed to each other (one describing man's conquest of meaning that is, as Thoreau says, driven into a corner, one describing man's conquest by meaning on which he is impaled), the idea of "fronting a fact" reiterated by both passages inevitably relates them, however they may occur at seven pages' remove, suggesting, I think unintentionally, that the cornering of facts is not triumphant or sweet, as both passages boast, but ultimately suicidal.

Yet the awe *Walden* inspires arises just from its insistence that what is essential can be winnowed to recognition, that facts can be isolated from the phenomenal confusion in which they are embedded, that in Thoreau's most extraordinary image, no longer elusive, life itself can be driven into a corner. The strategy for our salvation is one of excision, for the hope is that if Thoreau can pry us away from our diversions, he will edge us into a corner where only a fool would want not to be. The tactic of refining experience to what is essential manifests itself in a number of contexts: thematically in the book's insistence we relinquish what is gratuitous; in particular images which equate attention to a single phenomenon with penetration to a core, as in the image of sucking out the marrow; in the idea that two years of experience can be distilled to one. The book's economy is most apparent at a syntactic level in sentences whose didacticism comes from their epigrammatic sparseness. These sentences are often chiselled from a whole *Journal* reflection. I wish to consider one such sentence and its counterpart in *Walden;* so doing, we see how meaning in *Walden* depends upon experience which, as if driven into a corner, is rescued from the details that have engendered it, whereas in the *Journal,* it conversely depends on the way in which phenomena amass around each other.

In "Brute Neighbors," Thoreau asks, "Why do precisely these objects which we behold make a world?" (*W,* 225). The sentence stands apart as an isolated paragraph, although it will be remembered that it intervenes between the dialogue that the solitary figures of "Poet" and "Hermit" hold with each other and the description of Thoreau's other brute neighbors—the mice, the phoebe, the loon, the ducks. Although the question with which Thoreau startles us in *Walden* provokes the idea of our consideration of it, the fact of that consideration is preempted. Thinking about the question as anything but an aphoristic statement—meant to express wonder at the way in which the seeing of fragmented objects pulls them together—is exactly what we are not meant to do. Here, as frequently in *Walden,* questions are rhetorical. In this case, the question functions as a pivot, dividing the dialogue between "Hermit" and "Poet" from the description of the animals, structurally enacting the split to which Thoreau is pointing between the piecemeal nature of objects and the way in which our vision disproportionately composes them. As the description of the animals represents the former (is a list of incidental phenomena), the discussion between Hermit and Poet represents the latter, and is in form—the form by which its conversants are typified—if not in content, an indication of significance. In *Walden* the question (why do these objects make a world?) does not function as an interrogative, for it is dislodged by another question occasioned by the initial query's unexplained placement (why is Thoreau asking this question at this moment in the chapter?). We are further distracted from considering the question by the fact that Thoreau illustrates it—himself treating it as a proposition.

In the corresponding passage from the *Journal*, impressions have not yet been abstracted into objects. Moreover, they do not "make a world," they "accompany a life." Since the self is perceived to be separate from what it sees, the asker of the question is not lisabled from its consideration by its absorption of him into the whole he is questioning. The question in *Walden* ("Why do precisely these objects which we behold make a world?") suggests an equative relationship between the objects beheld and the world they compose. The question in the *Journal* ("Why should just these sounds and sights accompany our life?") suggests juxtapositions. It is interesting to think of what accompaniment means. It is a musical metaphor for the sound of the blackbirds described in the passage below. It also intimates companionship, suggesting that man, not fronting nature, has it alongside of him.[22] In addition, because the question in the *Journal* is not a self-sufficient sentence in its own paragraph, it requires expansion. The passage from the *Journal* entry is itself the termination of a lengthy meditation in which one impression verges on another. The questions in the *Journal* and in "Brute Neighbors" do not differ from each other only in their respective wordings, but also because one precedes a list of observations (and preempts a meditation) and the other follows a list of observations opening into a meditation from which it is inseparable:

April 18 Storm begins this morn & continues 5 days incessantly
The ground is now generally bare of snow—though it lies along walls & on the north sides of vallies in the woods—pretty deep— We have had a great deal of foul weather this season—scarcely two fair days together.
Gray refers the cone-like excrescences on the ends of willow twigs to the punctures of insects. I think that both these & the galls of the oak &c are to be regarded as something more normal than this implies. Though it is impossible to draw the line between disease & health at last
Day before yesterday I brought home some twigs of that earliest large oval catkinned willow just over Hubbards Bridge on the right-hand—a male tree. The anthers just beginning to show themselves

(not *quite* so forward as those above the Dea. Hosmer House which I have thought to be the same.) They looked much the worse for the rain. Catkins about 1 inch long. not being (much expanded yet) opening a little below the apex 2 stamens to a scale. There are smaller female bushes further on on the left—catkins about the same size with greenish ovaries, stalked & rather small & slightly reddish stigmas. 4 divided. I thought this the other sex of the same tree.

There is also the very gray-hard-wood-like willow at the bars just beyond Hubbards brook with long cylindrical caterpiller like catkins— which do not yet show their yellow— And 3dly opposite the 1st named i.e. the other side the way a smaller catkined willow not yet showing its yellow— —4thly near the Conantum swamp sterile catkins *in blossom* on a bush willow 1 ¼ inches long—more forward than any—but the stamens 1 to a bract or scale & bifid to trifid or quatrifid toward the top!! 5thly what I should think the S. humidis i.e. of *Muhl.* shows its small catkins now—but not yet blossoms.

I still feel stiff places in the swamps where there is ice still. Saw yesterday on an apple tree in company with the fringilla hiemalis an olivaceous backed-yellow throated & yellow-brown spotted breast about the same size or a little less than they.—the first of the late coming or passing—or the summer birds? When we have got to these colors the olivaceous & yellow—then the sun is high in the sky. The fringilla hiemalis is the most common bird at present.

Was pleased to observe yesterday in the woods a new method (to me) which the wood chopper had invented to keep up his corded wood—where he could not drive a stake on account of the frost. He had set up the stake on the surface—then looped several large birch withes once about it—resting the wood on their ends—as he carried up the pile—or else he used a fork stick—thus—

2 Pm to River

A driving rain i.e. a rain with Easterly wind & driving mists. River higher than before this season—about 18 inches of the highest arch of the stone arch above water. Going through Dennis' field with C. saw a flock of geese on E. side of river near willows. 12 great birds on the troubled surface of the meadow delayed by the storm. We lay on the ground behind an oak & our umbrella 80 rods off & watched them. Soon we heard a gun go off but could see no smoke in the mist & rain. & the whole flock rose spreading their great wings & flew with clangor a few rods & lit in the water again—then swam

swiftly toward our shore—with outstretched necks. I knew them first
from ducks by their long necks. Soon appeared the man running
toward the shore in vain in his great coat. But he soon retired in
vain. We remained close under our umbrella by the tree—ever and
anon looking through a peep hole between the umbrella & the tree
at the birds—on they came, sometimes in 2 sometimes in 3 squads—
warily—till we could see the steel blue & green reflections from their
necks. (?) We held the dog close the while C lying on his back in the
rain had him in his arms.—and thus we gradually edged round on
the ground in this cold wet windy storm keeping our feet to the tree
& the great wet calf of a dog with his eyes shut so meekly in our
arms. We laughed well at our adventure. They swam fast. &
warily—seeing our umbrellas occasionally one expanded a grey
wing. They showed white on breasts. And not till after half an
hour—sitting cramped & cold & wet on the ground did we leave
them. Ducks also were on the meadow. I have seen more ducks
within a few days than ever before. They are apparently delayed
here by the backwardness of the season. Yesterday the river was full
of them. It proves a serious storm—the point of pines left by Britton
on Hubbard's meadow. looks very dark in the mist. We cannot see
more than 80 rods before as we walk. Saw a size able hawk in the
meadow at N meadow crossing with a white rump—(the hen-har-
rier(?)) The catkins of the Alnus incana at Jennie's Brook are longer
than ever—3 or 4 inches. Some body keeps his minnows there in a
barrel— Observed a thistle just springing up in the meadows—a disk
of green a few inches in diameter in the midst of the old decayed
leaves—which now being covered with rain drops beaded—& edged
the close packed leaves *with purple* made a very rich sight not to be
seen in dry weather— The green leaves of the thistle in a dense disk
edged with purple & covered with bead-like rain drops—just springing from the meadow It reminded me of some delicious fruit—all
ripe—quite flat.— We sought the desert it is so agreeable to cross
the sand in wet weather. You might dig into the sand for dryness. I
saw where somebody appeared to have dug there for turtles eggs.
The catkins of some willows—silvery & not yet blossomed—covered
with rain-like dew look like snow or frost—sleet adhereing to the
twigs. The andromeda in Tarbells swamp—does not look so fresh—
nor red now— Does it require a sunny day? The buds of the balm of
gilead coated with a gummy substance—mahogany (?) colored have
already a fragrant odor— Heard the cackling of geese from over the
ministerial swamp & soon appeared 28 geese that flew over our
heads toward the other river we had left— we now near the Black

birches. With these great birds in it the air seems for the first time inhabited. We detect holes in their wings. Their Clank expresses anxiety.

The most interesting fact perhaps at present is these tender yellow blossoms these half expanded sterile aments of the willow—seen through the rain & cold signs of the advancing year—pledges of the sun's return. Anything so delicate both in structure in color & in fragrance contrasts strangely with surrounding nature & feeds the faith of man. The fields are acquiring a greenish tinge.

The birds which I see & hear in the midst of the storm are robins— song sparrows blackbirds and crows occasionally.

This is the spring of the year— Birds are migrating northward to their breeding places; the melted snows are escaping to the sea. We have now the unspeakable rain of the Greek winter. The element of water prevails. The river has far overflown its channel. What a conspicuous place nature has assigned to the skunk cabbage—first flower to show itself above the bare ground! What occult relation is implied between this plant & man? Most buds have expanded perceptibly— show some greenness or yellowness. Universally nature relaxes some what of her rigidity— yields to the influence of heat. Each day the grass springs & is greener. The skunk cabbage is inclosed in its spathe but the willow catkin expands its bright yellow blossoms without fear at the end of its twigs. & the fertile flower of the hazel—has elevated its almost invisible crimson star of stigmas above the sober & barren earth.

The sight of the sucker floating on the meadow at this season affects me singularly. as if it were a fabulous or mythological fish— realizing my *idea* of a fish—It reminds me of pictures of dolphins or of proteus. I see it for what it is—not an actual terrene fish—but the fair symbol of a divine idea—the design of an artist—its color & form—its gills & fins & scales—are perfectly beautiful—because they completely express to my mind what they were intended to express— It is as little fishy as a fossil fish. Such a form as is sculptured on ancient monuments and will be to the end of time—made to point a moral. I am serene & satisfied when the birds fly & the fishes swim as in fable, for the moral is not far off. When the migration of the goose is significant and has a moral to it. When the events of the day have a mythological character & the most trivial is symbolical. For the first time I perceive this spring that the year is a circle— I see distinctly the spring arc thus far. It is drawn with a firm line. Every incident is a parable of the great teacher. The cranberries washed up in the meadows & into the road on the causeways now yields a pleasant acid.

Why should just these sights & sounds accompany our life? Why should I hear the chattering of blackbirds—why smell the skunk each year? I would fain explore the mysterious relation between myself & these things. I would at least know what these things unavoidably are— —make a chart of our life—know how its shores trend—that butterflies reappear & when—know why just this circle of creatures completes the world. Can I not by expectation affect the revolutions of nature—make a day to bring forth some thing new?

As Cawley loved a garden, so I a forest. Observe all kinds of coincidences—as what kinds of birds come with what flowers.

An East Wind, I hear the clock strike plainly 10 or 11. Pm. (April 18, 1852 [10:721–729])

Noting the entry's focus on the signs of spring fails to account for what other concerns catch our attention and seem irrelevant to the dominant subject of the season's changing. I am thinking of the passage in which rain pours down on Thoreau and his friend (Channing) who are at once part of the scene and voyeuristically taking stock of it—Thoreau here stressing the senselessness of the venture and the intensity of its perusal. Or the passage in which Thoreau designates a storm as "serious"—a nomination generated not by how it affects us but rather by criteria made to seem more critical: "Ducks also were on the meadow . . . They are apparently delayed here by the backwardness of the season. It proves a serious storm." Or the sentence which documents just that moment when birds are viewed in the sky, making it appear "for the first time inhabited." That these moments should be notable has something to do with the way in which Thoreau both specifies significance and connects it only tangentially to human or didactic considerations.

In lieu of conventionally dictated foci, we are prevented from easy assurance about how to describe the entry's subjects. The account moves from the perception of the diseases of trees, to a catalogue of willows, to the observation that one species is in blossom; then that the ice is thawing; then to the recollection of an outing in which Thoreau is drenched, and in which twenty-eight geese are seen overhead; to Thoreau's attention to the wetness of the sand; to the general dominance of water (hence to a description of the skunk flower—the first blossom of spring) and of the sucker, which looks more like the idea of a fish than an actual fish; to the difference between what is real and what is mythological, thus leading Thoreau to think that sights are really morals. But morals of what? This provokes the question of what it means to see; to be related to what one sees; to expect certain visions; to surmise that expectation and creation may be connected. If we pay attention to the passage's end we are struck by the emerging thematic unity in the sentences, signaling as they do the perception of spring's arrival or the fact that spring's arrival occasions questions about meaning. Unity is expressed most forcefully in the idea of accompaniment (man's life with expectations of natural phenomena). We are simultaneously struck by the pointlessness of the concluding observations, for the sights and sounds which accompany man's life seem no more and no less than a series of impressions which add up to nothing by not being aimed toward cumulative meaning. The cynical interpretation of the "pointlessness" I am describing is that it is not an appearance. But in this particular entry, as the last paragraph considers the manner of noting phenomena we might wish to explain as arbitrary (says they are "coincidental"), it disallows, by itself commenting upon, and so making part of its subject, that interpretation.

The effect of stating the moral is to call it into question. What is the moral, anyway? That nature has an order? That it is cyclical rather than progressive? That the eye makes meanings, is, as Emerson said, the first circle? That it makes the sight of the fish into the idea of the fish, abstracts from what it sees? Conceptualizes as well as feels? That incidents are not random but are rather parabolic? Hence the fish is a symbol (objects are symbols), the year is a circle (seasons make a whole), there is an occult relation between the skunk cabbage and the man (between nature and man)? Then why does the statement of the moral initiate questions? It is, after all, as if the confidence of the assertion that sights have meanings (are not, as it seemed, a product of where the eye lights by chance) breaks off at the ability to retain or to know what

that meaning would be. Thus we see a progression from the
assurance of conclusions:

For the first time I perceive this spring that the year is a circle— I see
distinctly the spring arc thus far. It is drawn with a firm line. Every
incident is a parable of the great teacher.

to an illustration of the way in which incidents shore up meaning:

The cranberries washed up in the meadows & into the road on the
causeways now yields a pleasant acid.

to an arrested certainty of what those meanings are:

Why should just these sights & sounds accompany our life? Why
should I hear the chattering of blackbirds—why smell the skunk each
year? I would fain explore the mysterious relation between myself &
these things. I would at least know what these things unavoidably
are— —make a chart of our life—know how its shores trend—that
butterflies reappear & when—know why just this circle of creatures
completes the world. Can I not by expectation affect the revolutions of
nature—make a day to bring forth some thing new?

How we understand the structure of the *Journal* entry and of
the *Journal* itself depends on how we understand the meaning
of its concluding questions. In the process of determining that
meaning is not visible—cannot be read from afar (sculpted on
mountain tops), cannot be read close up (washed up with the
cranberries), the very idea of the circle on which discovery was
thought to depend is transferred from the visible arc of the
year to a different notion of completion, to what Thoreau calls
"revolutions," not reconstructed but made. Because Thoreau
sees that meanings are neither stably emblematic nor single, he
understands the importance of fidelity to detail—hence the renunciation of the symbolic abstraction on which the *Journal*
entry, for a moment, pinned its hopes. To mythologize experience is not simply to abstract it, but, so doing, to falsify it: (1)
by making a single emblem (a so-called fossil-fish) of phenomena that differ from each other, and which can therefore only

be forced into symmetry, and (2) by suggesting that meaning is independent of the self who observes it—that is, by predicating discrete vision on the sacrifice of relation between nature and the mind but for whose existence meaning is immaterial.

How the self comes together with phenomena in the world is always an accident out of which significance is gleaned. Thus Thoreau ends by attesting to the "coincidence" which characterizes the entry as a whole, and from which the desire for "pointedness" or a moral only momentarily departs. I infer a return to the waywardness of the initial pages of the entry from the successive questions with which the entry ends; from the resolve to observe "all kinds of coincidences"; and from the final sentence which points to the discrepancy between the distinctness of the phenomenal world and its accompanying indecipherability, as Thoreau hears the clock strike "plainly ten or eleven." The shift in attention from the fact of meaning to its coincidence raises the right questions about what is being brought together, and the word "coincidence" in the entry's last line cannot properly be construed to refer to any single conjunction. On the most obvious level, it refers to the connection of a phenomenon with itself (as in the striking of the clock plainly ten or eleven) and to the conjunction of one phenomenon with another (as in the chattering of the blackbirds and the smell of the skunk). Applied to man's perception of natural phenomena, "coincidence" raises the question of relation itself. For the "mystery of relation" between nature and the self inheres not simply in the sense that certain phenomena, themselves incomplete, arbitrarily engage and complete man's attention (this is the emphasis of the question as we recall it from *Walden:* "Why do precisely these objects which we behold make a world?"); it rather inheres in the inexplicable way in which ostensibly the same phenomena exhibit—at each occurrence—different manifestations.

In the context of the whole passage, then, the emphasis of the question is not on the discrepancy between the partiality of sights and the wholeness to which we convert them; it is rather on the particularity of sights, on why these sounds and sights, at any given moment, tug at us with their meaning, a question exactly parallel to the one we might ask about the material in the *Journal* entry. As these questions which conclude the journal entry suggest that phenomena do not remain static, in fact or in our perception of them, such phenomena also evade morals or interpretations because unlike even transient lessons conferred by fugitive impressions, morals are fixed. Even where "moral" means "parable" rather than "ethical example," nature shies away from such rigidifications. Because nature has no fixed meanings, there would be no way to settle man's relation to it and no way, as well, to disavow it as central. To be accompanied by nature is simply to have to see it: "You might say of a philosopher that he was in this world as a spectator" (4:251). I understand the sustained documentation of the *Journal* as the strategy for writing about nature that resists being symbolic.[23]

Thoreau comments explicitly on the persistence of his labor, noting as well the condescension it elicits: "I see that my neighbors look with compassion on me, that they think it is a mean and unfortunate destiny which makes me to walk in these fields and woods so much and sail on this the river alone. But so long as I find here the only real elysium, I cannot hesitate in my choice. My work is writing . . . [*and*] no experience is too trivial for me. . . ." "That we may behold the panorama of life with this slight improvement or change," Thoreau writes on October 18, 1856 (IX:121). "This is what we sustain life for." Finally on October 21, 1857, three years after the publication of *Walden*, Thoreau addresses the centrality of the labor I have been describing: "Is not the poet bound to write his own biography? Is there any other work for him but a good journal?" (X:115). These remarks could not be more explicit about the status of the *Journal* as it exemplifies a series of repetitions, hyperbolically designated as the poet's only work. For whatever gestures the *Journal* makes toward the idea of emblems, whatever the volumes *say* about generalization or about the wish to embrace symbols and morals, what the volumes *do* is to dismiss the belief that any fixity—of objects or our representations of them—could withstand or accommodate the changes in nature.

In light of Thoreau's remarks dismissing the idea of stable identity, what does it mean "to see what things unavoidably are"? Perhaps the idea of inevitability attaches not to the sense of fixed identity but oppositely to the sense that as identities are not stable, as change is part of what things unavoidably are, it is necessary to "make a chart of our life—how its shores trend—that butterflies reappear & when—know why just this circle of creatures completes the world." What is "unavoidable" are the permutations of phenomena, of which one therefore needs to *continue* to keep track. On February 12, 1851, Thoreau urges: "I would say to the orator and poet Flow freely & *lavishly* as a brook that is full—without stint—perchance I have stumbled upon the origin of the word lavish" (5:359). Further, he observes: "I can hardly believe that there is so great a difference between one year & another as my journal shows" (September 12, 1851 [7:116]). The keeping of a journal establishes credibility. To know "that butterflies reappear" must each year be tested and of when kept track. In the idea of "unavoidability" and the idea of "revolution," the sameness of phenomena and the mystery of their transformation are held against each other. These two concepts account for the tension which characterizes the passage's end and the *Journal* as a whole.

II

"What subtile differences between one season and another!" Thoreau writes on June 19, 1852 (IV:117). "The seasons admit of infinite degrees in their revolutions." On August 11, 1853, repetitive questions testify to the difficulty of correctly identifying what is being seen:

What shall we name this season?—this very late afternoon, or very early evening, this severe and placid season of the day, most favorable for reflection, after the insufferable heats and the bustle of the day are over and before the dampness and twilight of evening! (V:370)

On June 10, 1853, upon returning home from a long walk with Channing:

What shall this great wild tract over which we strolled be called? Many farmers have pastures there, and wood-lots, and orchards. It consists mainly of rocky pastures. It contains what I call the Boulder

Field, the Yellow Birch Swamp, the Black Birch Hill, the Laurel Pasture, the Hog-Pasture, the White Pine Grove, the Easterbrooks Place, the Old Lime-Kiln, the Lime Quarries, Spruce Swamp, the Ermine Weasel Woods; also the Oak Meadows, the Cedar Swamp, the Kibbe Place, and the old place northwest of Brooks Clark's. Ponkawtasset bounds it on the south. There are a few frog-ponds and an old mill-pond within it, and Bateman's pond on its edge. What shall the whole be called? (V:239)

If the first passage laments the absence of a name for the time of day (an absence predicated on the blindness to the existence of the discrete phenomena for which a name is deemed requisite), the second passage calls into question the adequacy of any single name to indicate the diversity of parts of the "tract of land" denominated as a whole. At times questions about names abandon interrogative form, as in the observation that "the river is but a long chain of flooded meadows" (April 7, 1853 [V:102]). Elsewhere we are told that phenomena may adhere to, or depart from, the prototypicality on which categories and names fundamentally depend:

A meadow must not be deep nor have well defined shore. The more indented & finely divided & fringed & shallow & copsy its shore—the more islanded bushes & cranberry vines appear here & there above the surface, the more truly it answers to the word meadow or prairie. (April 17, 1852 [10:717])

One could argue that in the previous passages, and in the discussion that follows, I use the concept of "name" loosely, conflating it, for example, with metaphor, periphrasis or literary circumlocution in general. I would, however, contend that Thoreau's concern with nomination dominates the *Journal* in ways specifically initiated by the study of nature, for if natural phenomena are not to be symbolized and if they repel analogic connections conventionally understood, Thoreau must determine how they are to be represented. On September 7, 1851, we are told, "Suppose you attend to the hints to the suggestions which the moon makes for one month—commonly in vain"; it will be "very different" (presumably more precise) "from any thing in literature or religion or philosophy" (7:81–

82). Thus Thoreau explicitly proposes the necessity of discovering a language to describe natural phenomena, much as Dickinson will propose the invention of a vocabulary to describe interior experience. To be bereft of a name or of descriptive strategies that would stand in its stead is to be dispossessed of the ability to identify the experience for which a name is deemed requisite:

> How hard one must work in order to acquire his language,—words by which to express himself! I have known a particular rush, for instance, for at least twenty years, but have ever been prevented from describing some [of] its peculiarities, because I did not know its name nor any one in the neighborhood who could tell me it. (August 29, 1858 [XI:137])

Thoreau's concern with the absence or insufficiency of names (because they fail to make discriminations between phenomena that are distinct, because they falsely make discriminations between phenomena that are connected) accounts for his interest in systems of classification. In the context of classification, it is not insignificant that Thoreau prefaces the volumes of his *Journal* with indices. What is interesting about the index headings is not only that they incompletely designate—fail to indicate the complexity of—the passage to which they refer (this we would expect of any abbreviation), but that crucial passages, which I consider in the rest of this section, are not indexed at all. These passages resist even the cursory designation provided by an index heading, for they ask us to consider phenomena definitionally evasive. In the passages I shall discuss, we observe not simply that phenomena change from one year to the next, as we saw in the previous section, but that they change more perplexingly as we are watching them:

> In Baker's Orchard the thick grass looks like a sea of mowing in this weird moonlight—a bottomless sea of grass—our feet must be imaginative—must know the earth in imagination only as well as our heads. We sit on the fence, & where it is broken & interupted the fallen & slanting rails are lost in the grass (really thin & wirey) as in water. (July 11, 1851 [6:561–562])

Grass "like a sea of mowing" seems a straightforward metaphor. Mown grass looks like a sea in its mass, its choppiness, mostly in its depth, and this idea is reinforced by the simile of the last sentence in which we are told the "rails" disappear into "grass . . . as in water." Given the directive to "know the earth in imagination," we can read "our feet must be imaginative," as proposing a true Romantic miracle in which man might learn to walk on grass as upon water. Yet something about the formulation is, in fact, more surreal, if less ostentatious, than the transposition I have just proposed. For to say that the grass looks "like a sea of mowing" is essentially to say "grass looks like grass" (the object of the preposition and of the simile, itself comprised of a genitive metaphor: the sea that is the grass), with tenor and vehicle always indistinguishable. The passage depends upon the divided inclination to see grass as grass and to see grass as water, insisting that when something is transformed it looks simultaneously familiar *and* changed. What is "broken" and "interupted" then is not just the fence rails but our sense of subjects or phenomena as discrete. At the passage's conclusion we are left with the impression that the fence rails disappear into the grass "really thin and wirey" (these adjectives, separating grass and rails, seem to modify both), and the grass disappears into itself, into that transformed way of seeing it in "this weird moonlight" that converts it to a substance neither entirely recognizable nor entirely foreign. The effect I am describing is not so much to make us aware of the redundancy of nature (the sea and the grass analogically brought together) as to make us aware of the disparateness of nature (of the grass and the grass analogically brought together)—with this concept a coherent one, the picture of grass bipartite or double. As in the last chapter, I here mean to emphasize that the point of the close readings of the passages at which I am looking is not to call attention to the ingenuity of Thoreau's metaphors. It is rather to demonstrate the way in which Thoreau employs metaphors so that, far from *establishing* relations, they rather call them into question—in this case, call into question the relation of nature to itself, of the grass to the grass.

Descriptions such as the one in the previous passage compensate for their disorientations first by suggesting that our accustomed mode of sight, as it relies on codified discriminations, is in fact a stylization from which Thoreau's redefinitions will rescue us:

The white stems of the pines which reflected the weak light—standing thick & close together while their lower branches were gone, reminded me that the pines are only larger grasses which rise to a chaffy head—& we the insects that crawl between them. They are particularly grass-like. (June 13, 1851 [5:491])

The passages at which I have glanced indicate Thoreau's propensity to see natural phenomena as transgressing against the conventional categories we would have supposed would legitimate them. The passages to which I now turn suggest that (a) although man is always inevitably connected to the phenomena he would name or redefine in lieu of a name, this fact has a different meaning when he sees his presence to have the same value as—to be no more or less than—other natural presences (when he is equivalent to other parts of nature he also registers), and that (b) in light of such muting of differences in which man no longer regards himself as central, he is commensurately unable to conceive of what he is watching as sufficiently whole or stable to be considered a discrete subject (something which can be delimited, totalized, if only conceptually, and hence ascribed a name). In this context the idea of delineating natural phenomena cedes to the impulse to see nature as piecemeal. (c) These changes (man playing a minimal part in his own representations; those representations themselves incomplete and subject to transformation) generate the attempt to see nature contrastively not against the background of human concerns, but rather against aspects of itself. The discussion which follows clarifies these distinctions.

In the following three passages we are shown what an object looks like when it is held against an aspect of itself:

Some distant angle in the sun where a lofty and dense white pine wood with mingled grey & green meets a hill covered with shrub oaks affects me singularly—reinspiring me with all the dreams of my youth. It is a place far away—yet actual and where we have been— I saw the sun falling on a distant white pine wood whose grey & [moss-covered] stems were [visible] amid the green—in an angle where this forest abutted on a hill covered with shrub oaks— It was like looking into dream land— It is one of the avenues to my future. Certain coincidences like this are accompanied by a certain flash as of hazy lightning—flooding all the world suddenly with a tremulous serene light which it is difficult to see long at a time. (November 21, 1850 [4:284])

The man looking at this landscape is repetitively returned to the coordinates of a specific geography—the shrub oak, the sun falling—even as his eye transforms natural objects into mesmeric ruminations about them. Thoreau seems implicitly to be asking why in the clarity epitomized by the sharpness of angles and exact points of reference, precisely delineated objects should nonetheless lose their focus, why seeing the exact juncture of the real and the imaginary should provoke rather than preempt questions about the actual. In the following passage, questions about a sight's status, whether it is real or imaginary, issue from the way in which the idea of the imaginary is not precipitated by thoughts about a given landscape but actually seems integral to that landscape:

The pines standing in the ocean of mist, seen from the cliffs, are trees in every stage of transition from the actual to the imaginary. The near are more distinct, the distant more faint, till at last they are a mere shadowy [cone] in the distance What then are these solid pines become? You can comand only a circle of 30 or 40 rods in diameter. As you advance the trees gradually come out of the mist & take form before your eyes. You are reminded of your dreams Life looks like a dream— You are prepared to see visions. And now just before sundown the night-wind blows up more mist through the valley thickening the veil which already hung over the trees, and the shades of night gather early & rapidly around.
Birds lose their way. (November 29, 1850 [4:301])

If the first passage balances the precision of nature against the stupefaction of our minds, the second passage balances the precision of nature against the stupefaction of nature, for the second passage presumes not to be about man's relation to what he sees, but rather about nature's relation to itself, about the question of "What then are these solid pines become?" One could of course argue that the trees' grading off to the imaginary is a subjective anthropomorphic conception. Yet there is a break in the passage a few sentences later which we need to respect and to take as an interpretive guide. It exists between "prepared to see visions" and the following statement which, though inaugurated by an "and" in fact has the meaning of a "but," for although the speaker is "prepared to see visions," what he sees instead is "night." Reiterating the notion that confusion is in the landscape and not in the viewer, Thoreau tells us "Birds lose their way," getting lost in the actual dark and not in the ruminated imaginary of the preceding sentences. The insistence that confusion is in the landscape and not in the mind reverses the picture of perception as the first passage presents it by suggesting that nature has imaginary aspects for which our dreams and visions are only oblique metaphors. In the context of nature's actual transformations— from mist to more mist to actual night—the analogy of the dream is not meant to call into question the reality of the transformation. It is rather meant to testify to the trees' disappearance and dissolution as we experience something comparable, at one step removed, in the dislocation of our minds. If the earlier passage juxtaposes the imaginary and the natural, this passage illustrates the way in which the imaginary is not just a way of thinking occasioned by nature (is not a way of thinking), is not a mental property but is rather a natural one.

The two previous passages do not present the same picture but they present comparable pictures of coincidence (of natural phenomena and our associations to them, of natural phenomena and themselves). In the following passage we see the gap created by the absence of coincidence between the self in nature and the self out of nature:

I feel a little alarmed when it happens that I have walked a mile into the woods bodily, without getting there in spirit. I would fain forget all my morning's occupation—my obligations to society. But sometimes it happens that I cannot easily shake off the village—the thought of some work—some surveying will run in my head and I am not where my body is—I am out of my senses. In my walks I would return to my senses like a bird or a beast. What business have I in the woods if I am thinking of something out of the woods. (November 25, 1850 [4:289–290])

"What business have I" is a pure idiom that in fact implies "no business at all" but rather the "rightness" or fitness of which this man is not now possessed. "Business," as work enters, however, through the vocabular back door of its primary connotation of "right" or entitlement, as well as by contamination from the social busy-ness Thoreau has left, if imperfectly, behind. The passage implicitly suggests that were Thoreau's thoughts *of* the woods (fitted to and fit for them) then he would have in the woods true business after all. The root word "busy-ness" travels in two directions, back toward town where business as transaction is severed from significance, and out towards the woods where a deeper, passive business might engage a man's attention, not incidentally connecting the mind and the body. Because one has to work at the integration described, being in the woods implies business or purpose in a quite specific sense. The woods offer a model for the desired reconciliations: for being in one's senses (being concentrated there) and for unconsciousness (obliviousness to that habitation). Wishing to return to one's senses "like a bird or a beast" which, in *its* senses, embodies the convergence of concentration and unconsciousness, means wanting the same kind of obliviousness as that had by an animal, and, as the absent (because gratuitous) possessive implies, it also means understanding that such a way of being is not a possession, does not supplement the self but rather defines it. Moreover, the fact that the meanings and connotations in Thoreau's passage only potentially coincide calls our attention not simply to the discrepancy between animal and man, body and senses, business as idiomatic "right" implicitly denied, and business as purpose implicitly affirmed, but to the equally problematic split between the frequency of such schisms and the mystification we experience at the question of how to heal them.

With respect to the nature he contemplates, man in general

is not so different from the man in the woods: because he is separate from what he sees, does not therefore see what is before him, because such separations raise questions about his own identity. The business of Thoreau's *Journal* (its purpose and its work) is to comprehend the separations proposed by the man in the woods—to learn why just these sights and sounds accompany his life—especially when he discovers that to be there in spirit does not in fact guarantee the knowledge of nature innocently, if implicitly, assumed to accompany him. Making sense of these separations, making do despite them, depends on acknowledging this simple fact:

I begin to see such an object when I cease to *understand* it—and see that I did not realize or appreciate it before—but I get no further than this. How adapted these forms and colors to my eye—a meadow & an island; what are these things? Yet the hawks & the ducks keep so aloof! and nature is so reserved! I am made to love the pond & the meadow as the wind is made to ripple the water. (November 21, 1850 [4:285])

The meditation on what knowledge cannot do opens into a revelation of what seeing can. We observe, though, more than a straightforward progression from despair to discovery, for the passage proposes a series of complexly related retorts to itself. We would think, like Thoreau, that the recognition that seeing and understanding are not complementary has no place to go ("I get no further than this"). But the very despair over the impossibility of the venture precipitates resourcefulness, as if the discovery of a dead end is cause to explore it. This Thoreau does in the sentence which confirms the earlier assertion that we impose what we see on the landscape ("How adapted these forms and colors to my eye"), know phenomena before the fact, hence instead of the fact. Yet such an acknowledgment prompts the remark that there is a discrepancy between our recognition of objects and our ignorance of those same objects still fundamentally foreign. "A meadow & an island; what are these things?"

We may interpret the question not as a return to the wished-for understanding relinquished by the passage's first sentence, but as Thoreau's idea for an alternative conjoining of nature and man—situated between the idea of innocent seeing and seeing in which the eye predicts and preempts "forms and colors." No sooner proposed, the alternative is dismissed by the "yet" of the sentence which follows it. As the first obstacle to sight lay in our propensity to understand a phenomenon rather than to see it, so this obstacle issues not from us but from nature, from what Thoreau calls its "aloofness" and "reserve." The remedy for our preconception was the replacement of the desire to understand with the desire to see. The remedy for nature's reserve is the following enigmatic sentence: "I am made to love the pond & the meadow as the wind is made to ripple the water." The sentence is enigmatic because it does not endorse the "sight" propounded in the opening sentence, nor the understanding initially rejected; nor does it suggest that we could answer the question "What are these things?" It rather proposes a new image for relation. But the analogy which would explain the meaning of the relation raises its own questions. Is love like the wind rippling the water because it involves transformation, suggests that how one feels about the pond affects how one sees it? Meaning what? That one sees it differently? Differently from what? Further disarming the idea of simple consequence: What is the connection between love and sight, love and understanding, love and identification—between the final terms on which Thoreau has settled to describe his relation to nature and the evolutionary stages through which it has passed?

Perhaps the real feat of the concluding analogy is to keep the questions it generates resolutely interrogative, specifically in connection with the crucial verb "made to," suggesting that its two connotations are as inseparable as the self and nature which, for unknown reasons, are wedded to each other. Thus the passage does not permit us to see a complete integration of nature and the self. Nor will it brook a segregation of meanings proposed by the verb that inaugurates their connection. For "made to love . . . made to ripple . . ." seems at first to mean "brought to" not "wrought to," where the force of "as" is "in the same manner as" rather than the looser "just like." The two senses of the verb, however (one a past participle plus infinitive phrase for "created to," one a passive construction for "compelled to"), build upon each other in a complicated mystery of first causes and present effects.

The discrepancies at which we have looked—between the real and the imaginary, the pine trees and the pine trees, the grass and a sea of mowing, man's body and his senses, the self as caused by nature and as immediately affected by nature—attempt to redefine the stability and circumscription of nature as a subject when man oversees that of which he is a part. Although in the passages I have discussed, man's connection to the natural world looks like an obvious one, Thoreau insistently articulates that this is an illusion. Nor is my point that, for example, in the entry I have just examined, the two connotations I attribute to "made to" illustrate an elaborate pun, with the point of the pun demonstrating linguistic elasticity. Rather, the two meanings call into question—and elaborate the quite explicit terms of—man's confusion about his relation to the nature he sees. The interest of Thoreau's figuration is not its literary versatility. Interest is rather generated by the philosophic investigation that lies at its heart. Man can neither name the natural phenomena he sees (where this means finding simple nomenclature for it); nor can he describe or identify those phenomena without acknowledging that divergence is integral to what is being described. Hence the explicitly unanswered "what are these things?" Finally, neither can he "read" natural phenomena, as the textual metaphor of the following sentence, written on November 25, 1850 (4:291), makes clear. While Thoreau may avail himself of the conventional notion that "A genuine thought or feeling can find expression for itself, if it have to invent hieroglyphics. It has the universe for type metal" (September 8, 1851 [7:94]), the mind stops dead at the uncertainty of how to realize this metaphor:

These expansions of the river skim over before the river itself takes on its icy fetters. What is the analogy? (November 25, 1850 [4:291])

Presumably Thoreau means to say that he sees those parts of the water that have frozen at the river's edge and only on its surface, before the deeper center of the whole river's solid freezing. Thus "skim" seems to mean not "slide" but "form a thin layer," in this case of ice. Although the two sentences I have quoted constitute their own paragraph, the paraphrase I have suggested is corroborated by the beginning of an earlier one from the same *Journal* entry:

I found Fair Haven skimmed entirely over, though the stones which I threw down on it from the high bank on the east broke through— Yet the river was open. The landscape looked singularly clean & pure and dry—the air like a pure glass being [laid] over the picture . . . ice on the water—& winter in the air—but yet not a particle of snow on the ground. The woods divested in great part of their leaves are being ventilated It is the season of perfect works— (4:290–291)

In the initial passage, Thoreau seems to be contemplating the way in which one sees the part (pieces of ice) before the whole (the entire frozen river), sees the ice floes before the whole river has frozen solid. But although the primary connotation of "skim over" is a skimming of the water's surface with a layer of thin ice, given the passage's concluding question (and the fact that in the context of the whole *Journal* entry Thoreau is reading the landscape as one would read a picture, reading it, moreover, in the exegetical context of God's other "perfect works") in "skim over" we also see that a metaphor has been transferred from the water to the man's vision. The metaphor is insisted upon because "skim *over*" also suggests something bodily or physical (unlike the spatial emphasis of skim *past*) with the added textual link to the river as a passage being read by the man, now in the sense of "skim" (reversed here) as a cursory reading of a landscape that will permit no deep or adequate one. In this subordinate but, I think, competitive second sense, we see the same kind of interpenetration and reversing of tropes that have characterized the other passages which would identify natural phenomena.

What is interesting about the interpenetration is that it gets Thoreau nowhere. In the entry there is no answer to the question, "What is the analogy?" We can only assume that there is no answer because there is no analogy, or none that, for all his facility, this reader of the river as a text can produce. The absence of an answer would be consonant with the other pas-

sages at which we have looked, as they have sought to describe, to define, paraphrastically to name the nature man sees
and his relation to that nature. They have in various ways been
defeated from doing so. While figurative language may command an ample repertoire to "identify" what is seen, in the
Journal such language seems ultimately at the same loss as the
literal language to whose rescue it has come. To put this in
different terms: the success of Thoreau's tropes raises the very
questions we would have thought they would clarify. Hence
where metaphors are invoked, they often seem self-cancelling
as in "grass like a sea of mowing." Or where puns are put to
work to connect disparate meanings, as in "What business
have I?," they stop just short of doing so. Where analogues are
enlisted, "I am made to love . . . as the wind is made to ripple
the water," they seem stalwartly evasive about the causality
they are explicating. Finally, as in the passage at which we
have just looked ("What is the analogy?") figurative language
is definitively interrogative, with the elaborately unexplained
metaphor, and the question with which it concludes, the last—
not the first—word on the subject.

In passing we might note the connection between Thoreau's
Journal, in which metaphor is so frequently ostentatious about
its ultimate lack of efficacy and Whitman's *Leaves of Grass* which
gives the same, if illusory, effect of having been purified of
figurative language. For Whitman, as for Thoreau, it is not that
figurative language is absent from the poem, it is rather that it
is made to seem either transparent or scarce. Thus the poem's
most memorable metaphor (grass as "the beautiful uncut hair
of graves") often seems its only one. The presumption of *Leaves
of Grass*, definitional and compendious in ways not dissimilar
to Thoreau's *Journal*, is that phenomena being described, in
need of no linguistic conversion, may adequately be named
"just as they are." Moreover, the question which occurs to us
when reading Thoreau's *Journal*, "Why is this being described?" (especially, "Why now?") also occurs when we read
Leaves of Grass, about whose concern with forms of order, given
its many editions, there can be no doubt. For the presumption
of both works, prodding our question, is that they are presenting totalities—of the world and of the natural world, respec-

tively—and that these subjects are larger than, different from, human and logical principles of order to which both explicitly oppose themselves. In Thoreau's *Journal* "Why is this being described?" (to which there is characteristically no one answer) turns into the question "What is being described?" (to which there is characteristically no one answer).

In the passage at which we have just looked, as in the *Journal* as a whole, Thoreau is not trying to find answers in the form of analogies between nature and the self but is alternatively trying, as he writes on May 16, 1851, to "Talk of demonstrating the rotation of the earth on its axis—see the moon rise, or the sun!" (5:416). Notwithstanding the brevity of the sentence, I understand the *Journal* centrally and repetitively to consider the ideas implicit in its proposition: (1) To examine the imperative commanding the conjunction of "demonstrating" and "talk." (2) To ask how such illustration (in this case, of the moon or sun rising) could be a "subject" in its own right, one in which multiple views of the same phenomenon are integral to what is being observed. (3) To insist that these phenomena are disassociated from human significance. Hence the impulse to liberate inquiry from the emblems, the names, the descriptions, the identifications, the analogies, in that order, after which we have observed Thoreau to strive. For man is in the natural world as its witness or beholder, not as its explicator. Thus the attempt to identify natural phenomena and to name them (manifested by one portion of the *Journal*) turns into the attempt to illustrate and to talk about those same phenomena (manifested by a corresponding portion of the *Journal*). Naming and identification presume that man, and his categories, are central to the nature that he sees; they also presume his ability to comprehend it. Demonstration and talk, conversely, avoid these presumptions.

In the following passage, also written on May 16, 1851, we see how nature looks when man is a mere part of it:

In the moonlight night what intervals are created—! The rising moon is related to the near pine tree which rises above the forest—& we get a juster notion of distance. The moon is only somewhat further off & to one side. There may be only three objects—myself—a pine tree & the moon nearly equidist[an]t. (5:416)

At the level of epistemology the statement is shocking because Thoreau fails to remark on how much farther the man is from the moon than the trees are from him. Yet the anthropocentric statement, with its violation of the scientific, is neutralized in two connected ways. The statement is made to seem objective, because once Thoreau has delineated his picture of relations, he has nothing more to say about them. They exist very much as a geometric construction would, disassociated from human affect. The statement may be flagrantly anthropocentric, but that fact has no interest for Thoreau and is put to no use. The anthropocentric aspects of the observation are secondly muted by what does interest Thoreau. For "the juster notion of distance" which prompts the observation depends upon the equal status of, as well as the ostensible equidistance between, the objects being regarded.

In this context, relation does not suppose connection—man to natural phenomenon—but rather supposes that one part of nature is as different from any other (that nature is as different from itself) as any one part of it is from a man. Thus Thoreau does not mean that in this poor light, it is possible to see only three objects. He rather means to insist that to arrive at a "just impression" of relation one must see as many as three objects, with the emphasis not on paucity but rather on a requisite number. The passage implicitly suggests that a "just" or accurate picture of relations—one with no omissions and distortions of focus—would contain two natural phenomena (to illustrate that nature is not an undifferentiated mass) and the inescapable, if unelaborated, human presence necessary to record it.

In the following passage we see the stick-like or minimal nature of the human beholder:

To lie here on your back with nothing between you eye & the stars—nothing but space . . . Who could ever go to sleep under these circumstances. (August 8, 1851 [6:670])

What is odd about the formulation is the way in which the infinitive mood paralyzes any questions about what is being seen. The strange grammar (the sentence does not say "to do this then . . ."; rather the infinitive becomes a question) immobilizes the man in the position ascribed to him, for it suspends his attention as if in imitation of the incomplete grammatical construction. As the previous passage took for its subject the position of relative objects (myself, pine trees, the moon), so the subject of this passage is the position in which Thoreau would put a man. Hence "nothing"—no distraction, no human concern—is "between you eye & the stars," which therefore constitute unmediated points. Although in the first of the previous passages man is in the middle of the picture, and in the second of the passages, he is one of its coordinates, in both his existence matters as a construct would. It is hypothetical or idealized, like that of a man on a "desolate island," in a passage to which I shall turn in the following chapter. Thoreau may insist then that a sense of "just relation" includes the human figure, but his own words come to life only when human presence is not its own subject. In the following landscapes, we see the absence of self to which the *Journal* aspires:

A tree seen against other trees is a mere dark mass—but against the sky it has parts, has symmetry & expression. (January 26, 1852 [9:449])

and

I observed that the white pines were particolored, green & yellow, the needles of the previous year now falling— Now I do not observe any yellow ones—and I expect to find that it is only for a few weeks in the fall after the new leaves have done growing that there are any yellow & falling—. . . . The trees were not so tidy then—they are not so full now. They look best when contrasted with a field of snow. (November 9, 1850 [4:259])

Although the perceptions issue from a mind—so we are shown in phrases like "I observe," "I see," "I expect"—we are simultaneously made to discount the significance of their origin. Putting it this way minimizes the complexity of Thoreau's maneuver, which involves getting the man out of the picture so as to enable him to compose it. By invoking comparative terms for which there are no specified criteria—"best" according to what? "Parts" differentiated from what?—Thoreau suggests that the differences in nature are self-referential. What seems to be at issue therefore is not a tree seen by man, but "a tree seen against other trees" versus a tree seen "against the sky" or "white pines" that are "particolored" versus those viewed against the snow. Even words like "tidiness" or "expression," wrested from the human domain, are neutralized in the passages, for in a natural context these concepts have no meaning. Perhaps this is because Thoreau makes nothing of the differences he sees. He thus implies there is nothing to be made of them outside of seeing them—the criteria for their assessment is *internal* to nature, and, by this fact, which we would suppose would make the observations pointless, he brings their distinctions to life. They come to life not because of their human significance but because any human significance that could be ascribed to them fails to account for the degree of Thoreau's interest in them.

Although Thoreau suggests "mythology comes nearest" to "an adequate account" of nature, "mythology," as I understand the word (like the morals and emblems discussed in the previous section), is predicated on notions antithetical to those of this enterprise, which rejects the idea of the typical, and of any story of identification which could be founded on a type. Hence the repetitiveness of the *Journal* years and of its subjects, for the idea that one year could stand for another, or one subject for another, implies the belief in the synecdoche that the *Journal*'s valorization of incidental "talk" and "demonstration" (opposed as these are to identifications and names, which reify the centrality of a human perspective) continuously rejects.

When Thoreau says that trees look "best" against a field of snow, although the superlative is borrowed from a system of human value, Thoreau's use of it here bears no reference to that system but rather disassociates the word from the context from which it has been translated. In the translation, "best" implies that time when trees look neither good nor bad, but rather most like themselves (not at one with our conceptions of them, not even most adequate to those conceptions), most clearly delineated from a field of snow, and, by implication, from all else with which they might be confused. Thus "best" suggests contrast stripped of the idea of value, or with value attached to the boldness of distinction between one natural phenomenon and another as it illuminates identity not through correspondence (between man and nature or between nature and itself) but by light of the very difference through which, at once isolated from us and self-referential, things noncommittally reveal what they are.

4

Speaker and Audience

Writing may be either the record of a deed or a deed. It is nobler when it is a deed though it is noble and rare when it is fine and clear memory impartial—distinct. Its productions are then works of art. And stand like monuments of history— (January 7, 1844 [*Journal* 1:494])

Walden assumes a primary hostility between the social and the natural; in recompense it posits a picture of man's union with nature which it extends to the social world as a reproach and an enticement. The *Journal* extends nothing toward us. It ordinarily evades the acknowledgment of our presence. As the *Journal* subverts analogic connections, conventionally understood (offers figuration which insists on lack of correspondence between nature and the mind and between nature and itself), so it also subverts a connection to an audience (fails to establish and so correspond to traditional models for an author's relation to his audience) conventionally understood. To invoke "convention" suggests that the problem is primarily literary or aesthetic. In fact it is practical, for though we are the audience for the work, we are in the position of not understanding the terms that contract for our attention. The terms are neither stable nor explicit, and I shall be arguing that Thoreau variously defines the idea of a speaking voice and an audience for his work; that he acts upon these definitions rather than articulating them; that we must therefore make inferences about questions as fundamental as whether Thoreau intends his work for publication, about our relation to a work that insinuates our presence and fails to provide for it.

Our connection to the *Journal* is, in addition, problematic, not only because it does not, as a published work would, take account of our presence, but also because the presumption of the *Journal* is that an audience and an author cannot exist simultaneously. We infer this exclusivity from comments in the *Journal,* which I shall discuss, that imply the author to be the audience for his own work. Alternatively, we infer it because if the work is not meant for a contemporary audience (if it is rather meant for a posthumous audience), the audience exists only once the author is dead. In the first case—when author and audience are conceived as integral to the work, the work presupposes no relation to us, for if we assume the privacy of journal discourse we are discounted entirely. In the second case—when the audience's existence depends upon the author's death (depends upon it rather than survives it)—the work seems not to contribute its half of the relation: all our suppositions about it and its author, generated from without, seem wholly external. Hence on opposite grounds, we have no relation to it.

With respect to the claim that discourse in Thoreau's *Journal* presumes the death of its author, I should here add that the argument in the following pages significantly differs from a deconstructionist one by virtue of its literalness. While deconstructionist critics would argue that all texts are effectively posthumous, because the text has an existence separate from its author and on this separation its integrity depends, the deconstructionists' metaphoric description of the relationship between author and text (words kill off presence) literally governs the relationship between Thoreau's *Journal* and his life. The *Journal*'s words have neither autonomy nor visibility—they are not published, and, I shall argue, cannot be published—in their author's lifetime. This situation (in which Thoreau's *Journal* cannot be published prior to his death) converts a condition of possibility (texts survive their authors) to a situation of necessity (this man and this text cannot simultaneously have life). I emphasize the point (a) because in the following pages I intend to explore the differences which I here anticipate between most texts and the *Journal* text, and (b) because one important consequence of the difference is that understanding the relation between author and text, with respect to Thoreau's

Journal, does not require the sort of shredding or disarticulation—of author from his words—on which deconstructionist polemics conventionally rely. Texts and authors may always ultimately be independent as deconstructionist critics say, but that independence does not necessarily require a literal death. In the case of Thoreau's *Journal,* I shall argue it does.

I shall, moreover, suggest that questions about the lack of relation between an author and his audience (or the revised understanding of such a relation) are inseparable from questions about Thoreau's regard for other men, especially for those others with whom he expresses kinship; to that end, I shall examine passages which talk enigmatically about intimate relations.[24] Thoreau's attitude toward others and his attitude toward the *Journal*'s publication have received considerable attention. In bringing the two subjects together, I shall, however, be suggesting they are only comprehensible when they are discussed in the same context.

In 1948 Joseph Wood Krutch asked a crucial question:

> Why . . . did Thoreau never utilize, or apparently have any definite plans for utilizing, the real riches of the *Journal?* . . . Why did he not at least plan the book which seems foreshadowed in dozens of the *Journal* entries; the book which would have described fully and taken as its professed subject that communion with nature which, even in *Walden,* is at best co-ordinated with, if not actually subordinate to, his plea for a simplification of existence, the purpose of which simplification being primarily the provision of sufficient leisure to make possible a "life in Nature"?[25]

Krutch thus observes that the *Journal* contains the book to which *Walden* is preliminary. I believe it is that book. Although Perry Miller was the first to insist that the *Journal* was a distinctly literary performance, he berated Thoreau for the failure of the venture, for squandering his talents on a work—this is the presumption—which no one would read. That the objections were evidently not borne out—Miller, for one, did read the book and in fact chose to write about it—would not have been lost on Perry Miller, though he never confronted the contradiction of his claims. Miller, moreover, chastises Thoreau for

being afflicted with a bad case of the transcendentalist's disease
in which the more a man loves other men the more passion-
ately he defends the importance of being separate from them.[26]
Elsewhere, as I have noted, he admonishes Thoreau for his
vigilant devotion to the "art of composition,"[27] a devotion
which dismays to the precise degree that Thoreau manifests no
interest in whether what is being composed communicates
with others. Miller assumes the first attitude (towards friends)
to be a bizarre literalization of a conventional stance. He assumes the second attitude (Thoreau's disregard for whether his
writing will be accessible) to be so idiosyncratic that its self-
defeating narcissism may pass without comment. Miller does
not see the way in which the two positions—toward his audience and his friends—are coordinates, for Thoreau's appropriation of a conventional attitude originates an important and
unconventional literary stance.[28]

In the following pages I shall discuss a connection between
Thoreau's expectation that his work will have an audience—
speculating that Thoreau supposed the *Journal* would see posthumous publication—and his attitude toward other men, specifically toward his friends. Thoreau's desire to postpone the
Journal's publication, to make it posthumous, and the idealiza-
tion of his friends, are, I would maintain, coincident. The confluence I am proposing is vexed with difficulties. It is therefore
easy to see why Perry Miller, to take the *Journal*'s most formidable critic, might not have connected the two subjects he considered. In being forced to discuss an author's attitude toward
his intimate relations, toward his work, and toward his audience posthumously defined as if such issues are related, as I
shall argue they here are, it can illusorily appear as if the critic
is replicating the confusion of subjects under examination. This
is true because the *Journal*'s redefinitions of audience and
speaker, which I will address momentarily, are generally implicit. Hence the process of inferring meaning can seem equivalent to the process of producing it. It is true because, since
Thoreau's cryptic statements require substantial explication,
the critic's descriptions can sound as fey and evasive as the
statements they are unknotting. At the same time, it is true

because in worrying the meaning of ostensibly precise statements, the critic may appear to sophisticate rather than to untie
Thoreau's aphoristic statements.

Yet as with the apparently straightforward assertions I examined in chapters two and three, which, upon scrutiny, elicited
our recognition of analogic language that conveys the simulta-
neous impression of discontinuity and redundancy, Thoreau's
allusions to his audience and his friends are characterized by
doubleness of reference, by an interweaving of subjects we
would have thought to be incompatible, and by the consequent
embroilment of the reader in their perplexities. While any
reader presented with the enigma of gnomic passages wishes
to produce explanations which cleanly demark one subject
from another, simplicity and separation are prohibited by the
Journal's overwhelming amount of material (the disjunction between the epigrammatic assertions I shall consider and the
Journal's massive length is itself disconcerting because, as I
have noted in the first chapter, to accommodate the consideration of each, incompatible foci seem simultaneously required);
by its conjoining of subjects we conceive of as discrete; by the
distinctions I shall suggest it draws between the idea of the
social and the idea of the human, and the connections it commensurately makes between conceptions about a speaker and
an audience—subjects to which I directly turn.

"The man who is dissatisfied with himself—what can he not
do?" (November 23, 1850 [4:288]), Thoreau writes, addressing
his own ambition. Dissatisfaction is instigated not simply by
those characteristics of the self seen to be deficient, but by the
very possession of a self defined wholly by human characteristics. The man who is dissatisifed with a self can, however,
disregard it, thereby clearing the way for another investigation.
Desiring to annihilate any personally distracting characteristics,
Thoreau speaks in the *Journal* of a longed-for transcendence in
which the speaker is sheer medium, "absent" from his speech.
To the extent that grammar permits such redefinition, in the
Journal, unlike *Walden*—in which Thoreau informs us he must
talk about himself because his is the only experience of which
he possesses knowledge—it is not the first person who is

speaking. It is the consequent phenomenological complexity, the sense of a speaker not recording much that is personal— not his work in the pencil factory, not his quarrels with Emerson, not the trial of his finances, not his writings for the *Dial*— and who commensurately posits a world from which an audience has been banished (for an audience, like a self, would have distracting personal characteristics) that constitutes the central fiction of Thoreau's *Journal*.[29]

The wholesale obliteration of egotistical aspirations leaves the mind vacant, and, in the following passage, we are told that a self-cancelled state is exactly what is desired: "The peculiarity of a work of genius is the absence of the speaker from his speech— He is but the medium. You behold a perfect work, but you do not behold the worker. I read its page but it is as free from any man that can be—remembered as an impassable desert" (January 27, 1852 [9:452]). It is tempting to trivialize the statement by imagining it evokes a metaphor for literary work distinguished by artless appearance. But from the occasions in the *Journal* in which Thoreau speaks of himself as a scribe and a recorder, we know that for him the emphasis is on the word "medium." The self has not been obliterated. It has rather been blocked from view, from its own view and from that of others. The idea of impassability is like that of repression. It is not therefore an accident that in the image of the "impassable desert" the connotations of intraversability and blankness reinforce each other in a double cancellation.

To put it this way, however, is to ignore Thoreau's equivocation about the self's relation to what is recorded. On January 10, 1851: "I would fain keep a journal which should contain those thoughts & impressions which I am most liable to forget that I have had Which would have, in one sense the greatest remoteness—in another the greatest nearness, to me" (5:341). If Thoreau would dispense with aspects of a self that are personal, he would preserve the idea of a self purified of its own features:

My shadow has the distinctness of a 2nd person—a certain black companion bordering on the imp—and I ask "Who is this?" Which I see dodging behind me as I am about to sit down on a rock

[No] one to my knowledge has observed the minute differences in the seasons— Hardly two nights are alike— The rocks do not feel warm to night for the air is warmest—nor does the sand particularly. A Book of the seasons—each page of which should be written in its own season & out of doors or in its own locality wherever it may be— (June 11, 1851 [5:477])

The passage has a double subject—the muting of the self and the differentiation of nature sufficient for the discovery that "Hardly two nights are alike," for there is an apparent relationship between obliterating personal characteristics and becoming attentive to nature's subtleties. Thoreau's enterprise seems one of exchange—an identity for an occupation, the externalization of the self for the internalization of the seasons.

Insisting that the self could substitute its attributes for those of the elements, Thoreau spells it out: "You who complain that I am cold—find Nature cold— . . . That I am cold means that I am of another nature" (December 21, 1851 [8:331]). The self, not dispensed with, is converted to "another nature" in the words of one passage, or to a "second person" in the words of another, and can see its own reflections as if from outside them.[30] In the separation of the self into two discrete persons (one who watches the self who in turn watches nature) the second person is foreign. "Who is this?" Thoreau asks. The second person is alien not simply because it is a projection wholly defined by impressions of nature, but because these impressions are then conceived as if they were inseparable from the elements they were recording: "A fact truly & absolutely stated is taken out of the region of commonsense and acquires a mythologic or universal significance. Say it & have done with it. Express it without expressing yourself" (November 1, 1851 [8:244]). In an imperative from the same passage, we are told that the man who undertakes such expression is "To conceive & suffer the truth to pass though [him] living & intact—even as a waterfowl an eel—as it flies over the meadows thus peopling new waters" (8:244).[31]

Though common sense is the medium through which elemental facts register, *it* is what is to be dispensed with. For the presumption about the second person is that his sense is not to be unobtrusive; it is rather to be absent, as if the identity of the self had not undergone reduction (the self limited to responses to nature) but rather redefinition (the self wholly eliminated or reconstructed as a repository for natural occurrence).

The idea that the self "reflects" nature, or is nature's medium, recurs in the *Journal*; on April 2, 1852: "it is not a chamber of mirrors which reflect me—when I reflect—I find that there is other than me" (10:658). On May 23, 1853:

The poet must bring to Nature the smooth mirror in which she is to be reflected. He must be something superior to her, something more than natural. He must furnish equanimity. No genius will excuse him from importing the ivory which is to be his material. (V:183)

And on October 26 of the same year:

How watchful we must be to keep the crystal well that we were made, clear!—that it be not made turbid by our contact with the world, so that it will not reflect objects. (V:453)

Expressing the self's obliteration in acoustical terms:

All music is a harp music at length— As if the atmosphere were full of strings vibrating to this music. . . . It is by no means the sound of the bell as heard near at hand . . . but its vibrating echoes that portion of the sound which the elements take up and modulate. . . . The echo is to some extent an independent sound—and therein is the magic and charm of it. It is not merely a repetition of my voice—but it is in some measure the voice of the wood. (October 12, 1851 [8:221–222])

On May 12, 1850, Thoreau elaborates the sense of the mind as a mirror, of consciousness as mediate, of the voice as expressive of an alien sound:

I noticed a singular instance of ventriloquism [to day]—in a male che-wink singing on the top of a young oak. It was difficult to believe that the last part of his strain the concluding jingle did not proceed from a different quarter—a woodside many rods off. . . . It was long before I was satisfied that the last part was not the answer of his mate given in exact time. I endeavored to get between the two indeed I seemed to be almost between them already. (3:143)

Consciousness does not just mediate or mirror natural phenomena; as we see in the following passage, the fiction of the *Journal* is that consciousness is displaced by them. Of a near expulsion of the self by atmospheric pressure, Thoreau writes:

> out of doors my thought is commonly drowned as it were & shrunken pressed down by stupendous piles of light etherial influences—for the pressure of the atmosphere is still 15 lbs to a square inch— I can do little more than preserve the equilibrium & resist the pressure of the atmosphere— I can only nod like the rye-heads in the breeze.— I expand more surely in my chamber—as far as [expression] goes, as if that pressure were taken off.— but here outdoors is the place to store up influences (July 23, 1851 [6:614])

Another image shows us how nature is at once internalized and recorded: "Properly speaking there can be no history but natural history, for there is no past in the soul but in nature" (March 8, 1842 [*Journal* 1:370]) Not just consciousness, then, but memory itself harks back to a store of natural influences— call them seasonal repetitions—for nature is the only history to which our lives keep returning.

Consistently, Thoreau admires those books which transact a substitution of the natural for the human. "Gilpin's 'Forest Scenery' is a pleasing book. . . . Some of the cool wind of the copses converted into gramatical & graceful sentences—without heat" (April 1, 1852 [10:642]), without being warmed by human considerations. On November 16, 1850: "In literature it is only the wild that attracts us . . . A truly good book is something as wildly natural and primitive—mysterious & marvellous ambrosial & fertile—as a fungus or a lichen—" (4:270). One year later, instructing himself on the creation of such a book: "Write often write upon a thousand themes . . . Those sentences are good and well discharged which are like so many little resiliencies from the spring floor of our life.—a distinct fruit & kernel itself—springing from terra-firma. Let there be as many distinct plants as the soil & the light can sustain" (November 12, 1851 [8:275]). It will have become apparent that Thoreau's images—a projected second person; nature passing through the self as an eel a waterfowl; the displacement of the self through atmospheric pressure; a self which orchestrates bird sounds by giving them utterance; a book filled with "as many distinct plants as the soil . . . can sustain"—internalize nature. However Thoreau's images shift, the presumption of the *Journal* is that nature is being spoken and by a projected second person, by a self redefined as an object of external reflections.

The self is not to be empowered by nature. It is rather to be converted to nature. We see the distinction between the alternative claims if we compare Thoreau's conception to the one in Shelley's "Ode to the West Wind," which dramatizes an apparently comparable desire to solicit nature's power. Shelley's poem voices the speaker's desire to be borne by the wind ("Oh, lift me as a wave"), to be played by the wind or to have it play through him ("Make me thy lyre"). In the image of instrumentality Shelley comes closest to Thoreau's conception of the relation between nature and persons, but the comparison is superficial. In Shelley's poem the image which unites man and nature can be analogized to nature ("Make me thy lyre, even as the forest is"), but the convergence of man and lyre, and of lyre and forest, calls ostentatious attention to its own status as analogy. When the speaker asks: "What if my leaves are falling like its own!" we are not meant to see the self converted to a tree but are rather meant to feel that, notwithstanding the difference between the natural and the human, the latter can be devastated by a comparable transformation. In the context of our question about the conversion predicated in Thoreau's second person, we will want to attend to the plea with which Shelley's poem concludes: "Be thou, Spirit fierce, / My spirit! Be thou me. . . ."

What is being coerced is the wind's presence or its spirit. Shelley's speaker does not urge the conversion of words into wind. He oppositely urges the transformation of wind into words. He wants the wind's demonic power with which to engender his own creations. He wants its power, not its essence: "Scatter . . . my words among mankind! / Be through my lips to unawakened earth / The trumpet of a prophecy!" The wind, far from cancelling human agency, comes to enable it, and to make it moreover accessible to others. And while Shelley's "Be thou me" covets the energy of nature, nature's energy is implored so it will awaken dormant human powers.

Conversely, Thoreau's "2nd person" subverts the very idea of the human. The subversion employs language which replicates the idea of personhood, specifying a "you" as well as an "I" (as in the assertion, "My shadow has the distinctness of a 2nd person") rather than language which repudiates it. In addition, without hyperbole or personification, Thoreau accomplishes that particular subversion of the human which involves the self's naturalization. We see that Thoreau avoids the language of anthropomorphism which would call attention to its fact, and that Shelley can afford extravagant personification because it never jeopardizes his desire to maintain his human powers.[32]

It is human powers in Thoreau's *Journal* which are presumed to be absent. This is true not only because the speaker is naturalized, but also because the audience, conventionally conceived, is presumed missing: "Speak," Thoreau tells himself, "though your thought presupposes the nonexistence of your hearers" (December 25, 1851 [8:346]). Whatever Thoreau's hopes for a posthumous reputation, his contemporary audience would have been unacceptable for the *Journal*. If we generalize from the examples of *Walden* and *A Week*, we see that imagining any real audience would have necessitated accounting to and for it. It would have meant incorporating the audience into the meditation. So doing, Thoreau would have disrupted the dialogue between the human and the natural—a dialogue whose first, whose only premise, was that discourse be private in the sense of unmediated. He will speculate on September 19, 1854, directly after the publication of *Walden*, on the essential connection between his solitude and his occupation:

I have given myself up to nature; I have lived so many springs and summers and autumns and winters as if I had nothing to do but *live* them. . . . I have spent a couple of years, for instance, with the flowers chiefly, having none other so binding engagement as to observe when they opened; I could have afforded to spend a whole fall observing the changing tints of the foliage. Ah, how I have thriven on solitude and poverty! I cannot overstate this advantage. I do not see how I could have enjoyed it, if the public had been expecting as much of me as there is danger now that they will. If I go abroad lecturing, how shall I ever recover the lost winter? (VII:46)

An audience for Thoreau's meditations is not, then, written out of being as a consequence of journal form, with the idea of "consequence" incidental. Rather Thoreau chose just this form because it accommodated his desire to dispense with an audience.[33] Having said this, however, I wish emphatically to add that the exorcism of the social—of the social, not the human—cannot be taken as an indication of Thoreau's misanthropy.[34] Thoreau's exorcism of the social neither proves nor disproves his feelings about mankind. Stated most simply, it has nothing to do with them.

The *Journal* banishes an audience so as to redefine it very much as it has redefined the idea of a speaker. Understanding the *Journal* turns on conceptualizing the mutual redefinitions. The speaker of the *Journal* is the second person, the recording consciousness whose sole function, we are repeatedly told, is to reflect natural occurrence. While it could be objected that by continuing to invoke grammatical categories I metaphorize the issue, it is exactly the point that the *Journal* itself specifies an "I" and a "you," so as to invert the conventional grammatical categories. Thus if the *Journal*'s second person is the speaker, is the access to the *Journal*'s subject, the "I" is the observer, is its audience. The *Journal*'s so-called first person is not the teller of its own story, but is rather witness to a story of preemptive importance, as we see in the following sentence in which the infinitive case blurs the question of agency, or rather repositions it: "To set down such choice experiences that my own writings may inspire me.— and at last I may make wholes of parts" (January 22, 1852 [9:430]). The audience for Thoreau's *Journal* is not absent from the work. It is rather internal to it— the I who will read what the second self has written. In this context, Thoreau's assertion that "genius is inspired by its own works—it is hermaphroditic" (October 10, 1858 [XI:204]) is not, as Perry Miller claimed, an example of Thoreau's damning narcissism. Given the muting of the self we have been examining, it is an example of self-effacement.

Author *and* observer, Thoreau will write and see written "A faithful description as by a disinterested person of the thoughts which visited a certain mind 3 score years & 10" (August 19,

1851 [6:701]). The "certain mind" and the "disinterested person" appear to be separate, corroborating our idea that Thoreau alternatively conceives of himself as a recorder of nature, and as an experiencer of those phenomena which have been recorded. While the implicit wish of the enterprise is that there be no disjunction between speaker and audience, first and second person, between nature and the self, Thoreau never falsifies the sense of relations. He may boldly re-situate them, removing the dialogue from between the social and the natural (where it stands in *Walden*) to the less mapped-out territory between the natural and the human. He may further suggest that a construct of the ego, a so-called "2nd person," can be the repository of natural reflection, but he then faithfully replicates the idea of disjunction between a first and second person, a speaker and an audience, between what he had elsewhere designated as "I [and] nature in me." What is to take the place of conventional distinctions (between nature and the self, between one person and another) is, as the following passage tells us, the production of mental pictures which are, however piecemeal, pictures of nature.

Certainly it is a distinct profession to rescue from oblivion & to fix the sentiments & thoughts which visit all men more or less generally. That the contemplation of the unfinished picture may suggest its harmonious completion. . . . Thoughts accidentally thrown together become a frame—in which more may be developed—& exhibited. (January 22, 1852 [9:430])

Such an invocation of others—of thoughts which visit all men—was just what we had supposed the banishing of an audience was meant to prohibit. Thoreau dismisses an audience, however, so as to internalize it, not only in the sense of specifying an "I" and "you" as integral to the work, but also in the sense of converting *our* outside attendance to inside experience. The *Journal* does not, after all, claim that Thoreau's experience of nature is exclusive. It rather stakes out the conditions under which that experience is accessible to others. To "rescue from oblivion & to fix the sentiments & thoughts which visit all men" does not simply involve securing Thoreau's representative thoughts; so doing, it rescues us from that immediate inattention or obliviousness to those thoughts of our own to which his record recalls us. In this important way, to elaborate a point, to banish the social is not the same as—is in fact opposite to—banishing the human. We are not wrong to understand the experience described in the *Journal* as conditional. But the idea of restriction does not denote a limit to the number of persons to whom the experience may occur. Restriction rather designates the grounds on which the experience may transpire. One cannot have the experience with another person, but that is not because it is not available to everyone. Its limits are governed by the fact that the experience occurs between man and nature rather than between one man and another.

There are, however, contradictions in an endeavor which reconstructs the idea of a literary venture so that it enacts a dialogue not between one man and another but between man and nature. In fact the *Journal* in its entirety raises the question of what it means to imagine a relation to the specific others we call an audience. If to imagine an audience is to adhere to the assumption that the relation to the human is a primary relation (an idea reified in literary works by provisions they make for others' comprehension of them) we have seen the lengths to which Thoreau goes to disassociate himself from it. In practice, he banishes the idea of others (either by speaking of their unimportance or by failing even to consider them) thereby insisting that the central relation to nature renders any others gratuitous. Hence the self ventriloquizes the idea of discourse so that as far as possible it is its own first and second person. But though Thoreau may redefine the idea of an audience (by internalizing it), a second and contradictory assumption is that a posthumous audience will be beneficiaries of this work. In fact one could speculate that Thoreau, like Dickinson, took advantage of the solipsistic conditions surrounding the *Journal*'s composition to compose in his mind an ideal literary reception. Then the wooden box in which Thoreau housed his notebooks would demonstrate the same cogent wishes for literary posterity as the packets into which Dickinson sewed her poems.

When Thoreau muses that he is unconsciously prepared for

some literary work but can select no work, when he notes, not without satisfaction, that he does "not know where to find in any literature whether ancient or modern—an adequate account of that Nature" with which he is familiar, when he supposes he might himself write such an account (he calls it a "Book of the seasons" and, on August 19, 1851, a "meteorological journal of the mind" [6:702]), when he insists it is "a distinct profession to rescue from oblivion & to fix the sentiments & thoughts which visit all men," when he speculates, moreover, that he would like to view his work from some future time "to observe what portions have crumbled under the influence of the elements" (and, by implication, what portions have endured), when he speaks of the high price of the creation on which he labors ("Sentences which are expensive. . . . Which a man might sell his grounds & castle to build"), we may infer his absolute confidence that the *Journal* will have readers. One could argue that these statements refer to *Walden,* not to the *Journal,* since they are written two years preceding *Walden*'s publication. But these are just the years when Thoreau, not revising *Walden,* is focusing rather on the *Journal.* They are the years, I would argue, when he is supposing the *Journal* to be the primary composition, a supposition I take to be affirmed by the fact that the *Journal* writing precedes and continues past *Walden*'s publication. We are thus in the position of being dismissed from the work and of having our presence presumed.

Thoreau's anticipation of an audience does not only turn on the evidence of what is done for or spoken about us. It also rests upon consideration of what is said on our behalf. For when Thoreau presumes to speak for all men our presence is coerced. That Thoreau shares our assumptions and so can voice our thoughts is italicized in those passages (I now consider two examples) in which men's likeness to each other and their relation to each other are said to be contingent. These passages thematize the idea of likeness (to another man, an author's to an audience, ours to Thoreau) and, as I shall suggest, simultaneously call it into question. So doing, they inadvertently make explicit our problematic relation to such assertions. Complicating the implicit claim that Thoreau speaks on our behalf, the thoughts which are voiced are not, in fact, ours, but (disabling the rejection of those thoughts) neither are they unrecognizable.

The following passage makes a connection between men's likeness to each other and their speech to each other, or, to put it as the passage does, it suggests a connection between the personal words of a speaker and the impersonal audience for these words—the unknown, anonymous (posthumous?) others:

> Though a man were known to have only one acquaintance in the world—yet there are so many men in the world & they are so much alike that when he spoke what might be construed personally—no one would know certainly whom he meant. Though there were but two on a desolate island, they would conduct toward each other in this respect as if each had intercourse with a thousand others. (November 9, 1850 [4:261])

The passage provokes two related consternations. The first concerns our identification with what is being said (do we, in fact, share the sentiments being voiced?); the second concerns our uncertainty about whom Thoreau is identifying (who are these others designated as recipients for the man's speech?). To address the initial question first: we, from the same evidence, would draw opposite conclusions. We would suppose that men are not like each other; that, insofar as they are, similarity should permit rather than prohibit intimate relations; that our definition of an intimate relation (men alone on a desolate island, to accept Thoreau's stylization) would differentiate our behavior rather than make it anonymous. On all three counts, then, Thoreau's suppositions are not just different, they seem opposite to ours—incidentally disproving the so-called likeness of all persons. We are taken aback by this assault on relations, specifically on logical relations, for, as I suggested, the very criterion that ought to enable intimacy rather suggests its impossibility.

Though it is tempting peremptorily to dismiss as pathological a statement that has dismissed our convictions, we are prevented from doing so by a suspicion that, at some level, our assumptions coincide with rather than contradict those with which we have been presented. It is not, after all, difficult to see the context that would legitimate the passage, for although the assertion transgresses against our conception of intimate relations by suggesting they are indiscriminate (possible with a thousand others), we also recognize that it is in our intimate relations that we most resemble one another.

Even if we grant Thoreau his insistence on our commonality, the passage presumes a mystifying connection between our likeness to each other and our lack of knowledge of each other. Does lack of knowledge mean that the man who is speaking does not know whom he is addressing? "Does not know" in what sense? Is it that he cannot identify the others to whom he speaks, cannot say who they are? Or does the statement also propose a connection between simple identification of another and deeper knowledge of that other which presumably under-lies the concept of identification and bequeaths it its signifi-cance? If so, how do we reconcile the idea of our likeness to each other and our lack of knowledge of each other, for on the face of it, these two claims are incompatible? Perhaps we would like to imagine them so, for even more disturbing than the idea of anonymity is the notion that "though a man were to have one acquaintance in the world . . . when he spoke what might be construed personally—no one would know certainly whom he meant," especially as lack of knowledge not only converges with the idea of likeness but actually seems predi-cated on it. To put the matter in grammatical terms: the "what" and the "whom" (the content of the man's personal speech and the identity of the man impersonally addressed) are rhe-torically parallel, and in fact it half seems as if the "whom" is not only the object *of* the sentence (as the man it designates is the object *for* the speech), but the reiteration of the subject (part of what is being said). Not to know "whom" is meant is, there-fore, to remain ignorant of what has been said, for at some primary level of identification the two are inseparable.

If coming to terms with the passage has its hardships, they could be articulated by the idea of stages: first, our wish to disassociate ourselves from an apparently repugnant picture of social relations; secondly, the recognition of the ways in which the picture is familiar (an association with the ideas we had wished to repudiate), and, finally, an ensnarement in a logical contradiction. It is just in the idea that men are alike and fail to know each other (for, as I have suggested, in the issue of identification knowledge is at stake) that the contradiction of experience replicates Thoreau's logical contradiction. We may wish to repudiate his logic, but we are unable to repudiate the familiarity of the experience the logic betrays. Thoreau's paradox is disturbing, then, not because we do not recognize it, but rather because we do. We are caught between thinking the causal assumption (that men should fail to recognize each other *because* they are like each other) to be unintelligible, and thinking that there should be some causal relation between our likeness and our recognition. Perhaps we fear Thoreau has discovered a connection, even as we are suspicious of its substantive articulation. We cannot counter Thoreau's assertion by the sanguine proposition that likeness and knowledge predictably accompany each other. We know the two parts of the assertion are somehow related, and not by a connection as simple as conjunction.

In the following passage, Thoreau appears oppositely to idealize human relations:

> I think of those to whom I am at the moment truly related—with a joy never expressed & never to be expressed, before I fall asleep (at night.) though I am hardly on speaking terms with them these years When I think of it I am truly related to them (January 4, 1851 [5:330–331])

The passage about the desolate island addresses the impossibility of personal relations, suggesting that men are identical to one another, and hence are unrecognizable to each other, that the "*likeness*" of one man to another, far from validating the idea of the personal, contradicts it.[35] The passage I have just cited suggests the opposite: that men can be like each other, hence truly relate to each other only in the absence of actual contact, for when men confront each other, the *difference* of one man from the other invalidates the idea of the personal by getting in its way.[36] The supposition of one passage is that likeness confers relationship. In the other, likeness cancels it. In one passage contact is prohibited ("no one would know certainly whom he meant") because all people are alike. In the second passage likeness is only possible in the absence of contact.

How do we understand the inversions and contradictions in and between the passages? The usual way to understand them is to suggest that Thoreau's inability to believe in men produces misanthropic expressions of whose despair we ought to disapprove. Another way to understand the passages is to suggest that we are implicated in ideas we would just as soon repudiate, for although we do not imagine that relationship can exist without contact, or that it depends upon absence of contact, we would have difficulty disputing another idea (one on which the disputed claim is predicated) that the facts of relationship and the ideas which sustain them are not in fact coincident.

Yet another way to understand the passages is, as I intimated earlier, to suggest that the identity of the people they purport alternatively to reject and to embrace is not obvious. The contradictions in and between passages, along with the skirting of reference—the talk about intimacy, for and against it, in language which evades indicating specific intimate relations—forces us to ask: Who might these people be? Perhaps Thoreau's evasion does not avoid naming particular persons (where this means not saying who they are) so much as it enables Thoreau not to decide who they are. One could speculate that in omitting Emerson's name in the passage cited above (it is to Emerson that the *Journal*'s passages on friendship are presumed to refer), Thoreau would have been calculating that the passage would be read by others, and that it may even refer to them. Why else excise the personal reference we would have thought the *Journal* entry was meant to establish? Evasions like these offer evidence more implicitly compelling that Thoreau intended a posthumous audience for his work than the field notes we are told he scrupulously revised. For the passages which sidestep nomination suggest that we are meant to generalize about the idea of human relationship, and perhaps to imagine an author's connection to his posthumous audience as a particular kind of human relationship.

What would this mean? The idea of "true relation" seen to depend upon lack of personal contact and the idea of speech addressed anonymously ("when he spoke what might be construed personally—no one would know certainly whom he meant"), while perverse if understood in the context of friendship, are entirely comprehensible in the context of thoughts about one's relation to an audience for work posthumously received. Although not every audience that postdates the writing of a work implies the author's death, in nineteenth-century America the death of an author and the life of an audience (the latter designated, as a matter of fact, to be friends of that author) is an absolutely conventional, and conventionally spoken-about, "exchange."

Exemplifying a traditional fictional connection between an author's audience and his friends in "The Custom House," Hawthorne tells us that "utterance [is] benumbed unless the speaker stand in some true relation to his audience." As the latter half of the sentence elaborates, "true relation" is one of friendship: "it may be pardonable to imagine that a friend, a kind and apprehensive, though not the closest friend, is listening to our talk." In the "Extracts" to *Moby-Dick*, the Sub-Sub-Librarian, ostensibly addressing the author of the book that is to follow, assures him of an audience at once sympathetic and dead—an audience whose sympathy seems contingent on the author's death, and, most pointedly, on the consequent relationships established not on this earth or governed by its laws, but rather succeeding them: "For by how much the more pains ye take to please the world, by so much the more shall ye for ever go thankless! . . . But gulp down your tears and hie aloft to the royal-mast with your hearts; for your friends who have gone before are clearing out the seven-storied heavens, and making refugees of long-pampered Gabriel, Michael, and Raphael, against your coming." Melville and Hawthorne blur the distinction between audience and friends, attributing to their ideal readers distant friendship and posterity, respectively. The fact remains that *The Scarlet Letter* and *Moby-Dick*, successfully published in 1850 and 1851 (published directly upon their completion), are sent out to prove themselves before a conventional audience, an audience of contemporaries in which strangers outnumber friends.

In keeping with the appropriation of a convention the status of which is never once at issue, throughout *Moby-Dick* as throughout *The Scarlet Letter*, Melville and Hawthorne avail themselves of postures of intimacy whose pretense is transparent. The author does not know his readers; this notwithstanding, he speaks to them directly, purporting when he does so to give their feelings utterance, and confidently to articulate his relation to them. So Melville's following incantatory questions in "Fast-Fish and Loose-Fish" pivot their argument in our direction and arrive without ado at a sudden definition of our only slightly ambiguous connection to him:

What are the Rights of Man and the Liberties of the World but Loose-Fish? What all men's minds and opinions but Loose-Fish? What is the principle of religious belief in them but a Loose-Fish? What to the ostentatious smuggling verbalists are the thoughts of thinkers but Loose-Fish? What is the great globe itself but a Loose-Fish? And what are you, reader, but a Loose-Fish and a Fast-Fish, too?

Thoreau violates the conventions I have been describing; he does this by eschewing contact with his audience. Yet Thoreau's failure to acknowledge us is in fact accompanied by the supposition—acted out (most minimally in the preservation of the *Journal* material) rather than announced—that his connection to us, apparently inviolate, will endure his death. There is, then, an inverse connection between Thoreau's refusal to acknowledge an audience and his expectation of relations with others who are, in the terms of one of the passages at which we have just looked, unknown but conceived (their likeness acknowledged by distance) and, in the terms of the other passage, known only in distance (separated by their likeness). These "others" may be friends or an audience, for Thoreau's assertions transcend (to put it one way) and confuse (to put it another) the distinction between friends and audience. So doing, they cross and, in fact, blur literary and personal lines. While Melville and Hawthorne discourse on the notion that their works require readers in posterity (again in the "Extracts" Melville will say: "Here [on earth] ye strike but splintered hearts together—there [in heaven], ye shall strike unsplinterable glasses!"), Thoreau realizes the postponement of which Melville makes a metaphor. While Hawthorne humors his readers by suggesting they are friends, the *Journal* literalizes the idea that readers and friends are one and the same. One of the most unsettling aspects of this work is its insistence upon dramatizing its relation to us—with the idea of relation unclarified by the recognizable terms of literary convention.

In distinguishing Thoreau's revision of the convention which conflates audience and friends I do not mean to claim that Thoreau, unlike Melville and Hawthorne, is dumb to the difference of audience and friends; nor do I mean to claim that Thoreau, in imagining relations without contact, is not, as assumed, covertly speaking about Emerson in such passages, or about the idea of friendship for which Emerson stands. I do, however, mean to suggest that in the *Journal* the enigmatic and disturbing passages about human relation make more sense if we take them as Thoreau's attempts to define—simultaneously—his idea about his relations to his friends and his idea about his relations to an audience than if we take them to be statements exclusively devoted to the definition of actual friendships. Yet if considering the passages, as I am suggesting we do, as operating under a double imperative, defining Thoreau's relation to his actual friends and defining Thoreau's relation to a posthumous literary audience, clarifies one set of problems (it explains the emphasis on distance and anonymity), it reasserts another.

The problem with the belief that one could speak about one's friends as one's audience, and one's audience as one's intimate relations, is that it confuses kinds of relationships not in fact compatible. The notion that you could treat your friends like your audience (have no relation to them) is clearly problematic. But it is equally problematic to assume that you could treat your audience as your friends. In the case of one's friends, as the second passage demonstrates, Thoreau suggests that distance must negotiate the differences which are manifest when actual persons confront rather than contemplate one another. In the case of one's audience, as the first passage demonstrates, Thoreau presumes likeness between an author and an audience, presumes rather than provides it.

Yet on rare occasions, as if forgetting the imperative that permits discourse in the *Journal*—indifference to a reader, the absence of a reader—Thoreau refers to that reader. On June 26, 1852, he worries: "I have not put darkness, duskiness, enough into my night and moonlight walks. Every sentence should contain some twilight or night. At least the light in it should be the yellow or creamy light of the moon or the fine beams of the stars, and not the white light of day. The peculiar dusky seren-ity of the sentences must not allow the reader to forget that it is evening or night, without my saying that it is dark. Otherwise he will, of course, presume a daylight atmosphere" (IV:147). Perhaps even more than explicit reference to the *Journal*'s readers, of which there is only one entirely unambiguous ex-ample, the rhetoric of the *Journal* suggests not just a hypothe-sized second self, but the actual "others" we call an audience. It does this through the texture of its questions ("Tell me pre-cisely the value and significance of these transient gleams which come sometimes at the end of the day. . . ."[October 28, 1857 (X:134)]) and its consistent directives, ("Go out before sun-rise or stay out till sun-set" [December 20, 1851 (8:329)]) for the speech is addressed to another, whom—in the grammar of its thoughts if not in explicit reference—it continuously en-gages. Thoreau's journal seems, therefore, to presume an audi-ence, albeit a posthumous one, and in so doing, and in being a journal, it exploits the contradictions (between the private and the public, between literary conventions and conventions of private discourse) inherent in Thoreau's double imperative. How does this work?

To the extent that Thoreau chose to keep a journal (and not, as in *A Week* or *Walden*, to produce a published book), the discourse seems inadvertently interesting.[37] But to the extent that Thoreau's remarks on the *Journal* suggest that he conceives of its execution as the fulfillment of a "calling" or a vocation (as I have noted, three years after the publication of *Walden*, Tho-reau writes explicitly: "Is not the poet bound to write his own biography? Is there any other work for him but a good journal? We do not wish to know how his imaginary hero, but how he, the actual hero, lived from day to day" [October 21, 1857 (X:115)]); to the extent that given entries structure the thoughts they record so as to seem to digress from and return to central points of interest, which are descriptions of nature (to the extent that these descriptions can be identified as "central," even as our contact with them is minimized or rationed); to the extent that a real audience is banished so as to be redefined (to be internalized in one sense, and conceived as posthumous in the other); to the extent that passages which delineate Thoreau's theory of relations appear simultaneously to refer to Emerson, to no one at all, to an unspecified audience in the future; to that extent we are implicated in this discourse. In these cumulative ways the *Journal* anticipates an audience and in fact talks to us.

There are reasons why we might not wish to attend to the discourse. Because as utterance half anticipates our presence, it, by the same token, also half ignores it. Because at times, although Thoreau presumes to talk for us, he in fact talks despite us—an avoidance that can appear equivalent to talking against us. Because of the extreme frustration of reading material whose author is cognizant of literary discriminations (how to make a subject available, as, for example, *Walden* does) which he chooses to avoid. Because however ravishing Thoreau's descriptions of nature, the idea of nature as an ultimate or only subject appears an untenable simplification of experience. Perry Miller's passionate attack on the perversity of the *Journal* is, I think, a direct response to Thoreau's manipulation of the *Journal*'s reader, and to the sadism of that manipulation. We note sadism towards the reader in the *Journal*'s unwillingness to relinquish the lure of descriptions traditionally unrecognizable—of friends, of an audience, of nature itself. For, as we have seen in the previous chapters, the presumption of the *Journal* is that Thoreau can record the whole experience of nature; that, in so doing, he can make the idea of contact with nature routine; and, going one step further, in a progression we may not be able to follow, can, by embracing foreignness rather than familiarity, generate passion.

We are most aggressively implicated by the *Journal*'s speech because Thoreau's descriptions of nature bring us closer to nature than does any other work of writing, including the writing of *Walden*. In fact, while *Walden* is Thoreau's exposure of a

relationship in public and to the public, a relationship legitimated by contact with society (shared with the social world as
well as soliciting its scrutiny, for in *Walden* Thoreau espouses
his relation to nature as a model for our imitation), the *Journal*,
with its circumlocutions and dead ends, its excesses and exhila-
rations, exhibits a relationship which seems both unfamiliar
and inaccessible: something we can view but cannot have in
our own right. Thus our glimpse of Thoreau's relation to nature—with his invitation to scrutinize his words an undecided
matter, or rather, a matter which continues to be decided in
ambivalent ways—seems to us at once illicit and unsanctioned.
Voyeurism is the right word for our perusal of a document
which is ostensibly private. That the content of the document
is a private relation (Thoreau's relation to nature) validates a
term whose application in this context might otherwise seem
questionable. Further establishing the term as an appropriate
one is Thoreau's complicated attitude toward the intrusion of
our presence. At once private and public (on the one hand,
detailing a relationship to nature whose rapture seems generated by its exclusivity, by the idea that it fills the whole world,
and, on the other, making room in that world for our covert
attendance), what this work violates most profoundly is our
sense of disparate categories—specifically our notion that privacy and exposure are incompatible with each other, for in this
work the dismissal of an audience and the anticipation of an
audience accompany each other.

Nor is the crucial issue (the existence of an audience, or the
discrimination of one kind of audience from another) ever addressed explicitly, as, for example, it is in Wordsworth's "Essay, Supplementary to the Preface," in which Wordsworth distinguishes between "the public" and "the people," the latter
implying the posthumous audience for whom Wordsworth intends his work. Thoreau, unlike Wordsworth, often seems to
assume such a distinction; he does not voice it, although on
April 16, 1852, we overhear his ruminations on the value of
preserving his work *from* publication: "How few who advise
you to lead a more interior life! In the one case there is all the
world to advise you, in the other there is none to advise you
but yourself. Nobody ever advised me not to print but myself.

The public persuade the author to print—as the meadow invites the brook to fall into it. Only he can be trusted with gifts who can present a face of bronze to expectations" (10:706–707). Not so explicitly alluding to the subject of publication, Thoreau will nonetheless, and in terms related to those of the passage just cited, distinguish between two kinds of antithetical work: "To please our friends and relatives we turn out our inner ore in cartloads—while we neglect to work our mines of gold known only to ourselves far up in the Sierras.—where we pulled up a bush in our *mt* walk, and saw the glittering treasure. Let us return thither— Let it be the price of our freedom to make that known—" (January 13, 1852 [9:388–389]). Yet, to extrapolate from the quotation, the price of this freedom (the freedom to value the *Journal* because it is not the printed book, and nonetheless to print the book we know as *Walden*, while insisting that the *Journal* contains the treasure, an insistence demonstrated by the dominance of journal writing, designated as the "poet's only work") is to display an ambivalent stance in which we are teased by an attitude which insinuates its desire for our presence and refuses explicitly to specify or prepare for it. Thoreau, then, inviting, even as he ignores our attention, establishes our relation to the *Journal* which will always be troubled by the question of its legitimacy.

I have noted that the *Journal* does not speak to us. In fact it insists upon "the non existence" of hearers. Nor does the *Journal* speak "for" us if to speak for us is to voice easily recognizable conceptions. As I have demonstrated, it violates our conceptions, suggesting that nature is a subject in its own right; that nature is the whole subject; that what is monotonous about nature—its predictable repetitiveness—is what is moving about nature. Yet the way it speaks to and for us is by speaking in our stead, where this means articulating sentiments antithetical to our own, and it thereby raises the question of whether representative speech and recognizable speech are synonymous. The latter question is reiterated by a number of works contemporary with Thoreau's *Journal*. We intuit the question in Emerson's claim that "in every work of genius we recognize our own rejected thoughts: they come back to us with a certain alienated majesty" ("Self-Reliance"). We hear it in Whitman's compulsive insistence that his narcissistic words, his "electric song," issues from our lips, or on our behalf. If we do not repudiate Whitman's claim, it is not because his words are, as he asserts, familiar. It is rather because (as with Thoreau's *Journal*) we are attracted by the claim that what is external to the self could be integral to the self—integral, not alien. Whitman's repetitive solicitation of us (his inability to speak unaccompanied by the claim that he speaks to and for us) is as manipulative of us, and of the idea of an audience, as are the features of Thoreau's *Journal* to which we have been attending. The presumption of both is that one man's thoughts fill the whole world, and can therefore be substituted for the thoughts of others. In Whitman's case substitution involves the assertion of the absolute equivalence of his thoughts and ours. In Thoreau's case it involves the insistence upon the absolute difference between his thoughts and ours. Equivalence and difference amount to the same thing because in both cases the idea of an audience is written out of existence so as to be created. In the renunciation of an audience, as in the idea of writing nature (presupposed by the formulations at which we have looked in the previous chapters) rather than writing about it, and in the forfeited preposition that expresses this idea, it is as if the notion of relation had itself been made gratuitous.

In raising questions about relation and refusing to settle them; in insinuating substitutions (that the *Journal* talks instead of, rather than for, us; that our ideas are replaced rather than voiced); in provoking statements like my own which make unsubstantiated (and unsubstantiatable) claims about presumptively shared assumptions, the *Journal* asks us to deliberate over the meaning of passages to which we have no clear relation. To be drawn to the *Journal* is to respond to its bait. Since Thoreau's conception of nature is unimaginable to us, we will settle for what it looks like, will pry into what it looks like. But if we are seduced by the *Journal*, we are also rebuffed by it, and on the same grounds. The idea of a relation to nature commensurate to this one—large enough to fill a *Journal*, sufficient to fill a life—is inconceivable to us. We could say that in enticing and repelling us, Thoreau's *Journal* is to us what nature is to

Thoreau—simultaneously drawing us toward it and disengaging us by its alienness.

Like Thoreau in another context, we want to know: if nature is the totality, "what do the thoughts find to live on?" For the question of "correspondence" as we considered it in the previous chapters (of nature to the mind, of analogies that are subverted), no longer academic, is pressing with respect to the problem of whether our thoughts and ideas bear correspondence to those in the *Journal*, and of how, in the absence of correspondence, we define our relation to it. What is challenged in the work is not only our assumptions about the mind's relation to nature or our relations to each other, but, preempting these issues, or constituting their foundation, our assumptions about an author's relation to an audience and our relation to him. What is challenged is the idea that we cannot have relations without contact—in the next chapter we shall see the ways in which Thoreau tries to free words of contextually and hierarchically specified relations—at the same time that at every moment of its utterance the work supposes and depends upon our attendance. "Certainly it is a distinct profession," we recall Thoreau had remarked, "to rescue from oblivion & to fix the sentiments & thoughts which visit all men. . . ." Commenting implicitly on the hubris of Thoreau's assertion, Perry Miller asked in exasperation: "But suppose the sentiments which visit this recorder multitudinously happen not to be shared by the generality of men?"[38] The divergence to which Miller points does not, however, invalidate the *Journal*'s claim; the divergence rather points to the conditions that govern the *Journal*'s existence, and which, not incidentally, define our relation to it.

5

Writing Nature

The reader who has been accustomed to expend all his energy in the launching—as if he were to float down stream for the whole voyage—may well complain of nauseating ground swells, and choppings of the sea, when his frail shore craft gets amidst the breakers of the ocean stream—which flows as much to sun and moon, as lesser streams to it— If he would appreciate the true flow that is in these books, he must expect to see it rise from the page like an exhalation— and wash away the brains of most like burr-millstones. They flow not from right to left, or from left to right, but to higher levels, above and behind the reader. (January 22, 1841 [*Journal* 1:226])

It is the procedure of literary criticism to imply a false consonance between what is being said about a quotation and what a quotation "says." However we may suspect the coincidence I have described, it is nonetheless the case that most passages excerpted for our attention seem to epitomize something, even if we think that what is being epitomized deviates from the critical interpretation that urges our attendance to it. In the *Journal*, however, the act of excerption seems not to confer emphasis but conversely to blur it. That the conventions by which criticism ostensibly discourses about meaning should be thwarted by the *Journal* is not surprising, for if we cannot answer the question, "How does the *Journal* name, identify, and understand analogues for natural phenomena?" and also cannot clearly see ourselves identified as the audience for this *Journal*—if the purpose of the *Journal* is to disable these clarifications—we will not know how to delineate the boundaries of a quotation, for we will not know what the quotation is supposed to represent. To quote passages from the *Journal*, then, is by definition to distort them, and not in ways consonant with all excerptions which, leaving things out, by definition leave them less. In the *Journal*, almost regardless of the content of the passages cited, the less material given, the less interesting it will seem. Nor is the give and take of significance as I am describing it contingent upon severing a quotation from material to which it is integral, unless one wishes to claim that the question of what is integral and what is alien are the precise discriminations which the *Journal* asks us to reassess.

In the following pages, I shall be suggesting a connection between the synecdochal act of quotation (which in the *Journal* results in a distortion of the whole) and the *Journal*'s advocation of "talk" and "examples" in lieu of traditionally defined subjects. For quotations (illustrations *of* the text) and examples (illustrations *in* the text) are both substitutions in which instances are asked to represent wholes.

On May 6, 1851, Thoreau writes in his *Journal*: "The ethical philosopher needs the discipline of the natural philosopher" (5:413). Thoreau seems here to be suggesting that what man can see is a corrective to what he should do. On December 12, 1851, the word "discipline" reoccurs: "I am thinking by what long discipline and at what cost a man learns to speak simply at last" (8:312). The following passages, which equate the study of nature with the keeping of a record, implicitly address the "discipline" that connects seeing and writing:

A journal is a record of experiences and growth, not a preserve of things well done or said. . . . The charm of the journal must consist in a certain greenness. . . . (January 24, 1856 [VIII:134])

In a journal it is important in a few words to describe the weather, or character of the day, as it affects our feelings. That which was so important at the time cannot be unimportant to remember. (February 5, 1855 [VII:171])

I omit the unusual—the hurricanes & earthquakes & describe the common. This has the greatest charm—and is the true theme of poetry. (August 28, 1851 [7:27])

In keeping a journal of one's walks and thoughts it seems to be
worth the while to record those phenomena which are most interesting to us at the time. Such is the weather. (January 25, 1860 [XIII:106])

The passages reiterate dichotomies not unakin to those between the index headings and the entries, to which I alluded in
the third chapter, between things "preserved" and things
"green," between what is important to remember but presumably impossible to remember and therefore crucial to record,
between extraordinary events which command attention, and
the ordinary (natural) ones which Romantics on both sides of
the Atlantic would have agreed are the subject of poetry. We
do not, however, know why one's connection to an ordinary
event follows not from one's recollection of it ("It is impossible
to remember a week ago" the "disproportion of blossom to
leaves," Thoreau had written on May 9, 1852 [IV:41–42]), but
rather from one's relation to it as this is established by keeping
a record that does not transfigure the event but rather leaves it
"green" and "common." The assertions also raise questions
about the overlapping of terms—the memory of an event, the
record of the same event, the prolonging of life (one's own?
that of the season?) and the idea of repetition, as the latter has
something, though not the same thing, to do with all of the
subjects ("greenness," "growth," "the recurrence of the
usual," "the keeping of a record," the subject of poetry) on
which the directives touch.

The following passages are concerned with how particular
landscapes illustrate—in the sense of exemplify, as well as in
the sense of provide visual features of—the memorable (but
unremembered) nature man sees. Although Thoreau uses the
word "picture" to describe nature seen from far away ("All
distant landscapes—seen from hill tops are veritable pictures"
[5:404]), "picture" is also invoked to indicate any natural composition. Thus, for example, on January 24, 1852, Thoreau
writes: "When I come out onto the Causeway—I behold a
splendid picture in the west. . . . When clouds rise in mid
afternoon you cannot foresee what sunset picture they are preparing for us" (9:440), with the "they" referring most obviously
to the clouds, but proposing a split-second double image of

"their" preparers as antecedents. Often landscapes are called pictures because they are "glassed with air" (July 1850 [3:204]).

Yet "picture" also refers to man's replication of the landscape: "What a faculty must that be which can paint the most barren landscape and humblest life in glorious colors It is pure & invigorated senses reacting on a sound & strong imagination. Is not that the poets case?" (August 21, 1851 [7:7]). What is to be reproduced is not an aesthetic composition, but the wildness of the landscape, "a wildness" Thoreau had designated, "which no civilization can penetrate." In this context, to return to the passage first noted by Perry Miller, and cited in chapter one, in which Thoreau compares himself to a bee drawing beauty from the landscape, we can see the man, intoxicated by the synesthesia of his vision, mix the metaphors that, like paint, will reproduce the objects of his beholding: "How to extract . . . honey from the flower of the world—that is my every day business. I impregnate and intermix with the flowers by transferring my eyes from one to the other." The viewer pollinates first with his eyes, then with his words, intent on making not honey but pictures. Notwithstanding the extravagance of the bee–vision metaphor, Thoreau's attention to the landscape is scrupulously chaste, in the sense of being vigilant to the precision of detail—a precision that customarily focuses on questions of perspective and light. In an example of the former:

From the hill, I look westward over the landscape. The deciduous woods are in their hoary youth, every expanding bud swaddled with downy webs. From this more eastern hill, with the whole breadth of the river valley on the west, the mountains appear higher still, the width of the blue border is greater,—not mere peaks, or a short and shallow sierra, but a high blue table-land with broad foundations, a deep and solid base or tablet, in proportion to the peaks that rest on it. As you ascend, the near and low hills sink and flatten into the earth; no sky is seen behind them; the distant mountains rise. The truly great are distinguished. . . . You see that the foundation answers to the super-structure. Moral structures. (The sweet-fern leaves among odors now). The successive lines of haze which divide the western landscape, deeper and more misty over each intervening valley, are not yet very dense; yet there is a light atmospheric line along the base of the mountains for their whole length, formed by this denser and grosser atmosphere through which we look next the earth, which almost melts them into the atmosphere, like the contact of molten metal with that which is unfused. . . . (May 10, 1853 [V:140–141])

and of the latter—of light that does not melt into the landscape but rather differentiates it:

A field of water betrays the spirit that is in the air— It has new life & motion. It is intermediate between land & sky.— On land only the [grass] & trees wave—but the water itself is *rippled* by the wind. I see the breeze dash across it in streaks & flakes of light. (July 1850 [3:204])

The following passage combines a picture of perspective and a picture of light:

Moonlight on Fair Haven Pond seen from the Cliffs. A sheeny lake in the midst of a boundless forest— The windy surf sounding freshly & wildly in the single pine behind you— The silence of hushed wolves in the wilderness & as you fancy moose looking off from the shore of the lake. The stars of poetry & history—& unexplored nature looking down on the scene. This is my world now—with a dull whitish mark curving northward through the forest marking the outlet to the lake. Fair Haven by moonlight lies there like a lake in the Maine wilderness in the midst of a primitive forest untrodden by man. This light & this hour takes the civilization all out of the landscape. . . . The landscape seen from the slightest elevation by moonlight—is seen remotely & flattened as it were into mere light & shade open field & forest—like the surface of the earth seen from the top of a mountain.

How much excited we are how much recruited by a great many particular fragrances— A field of ripening corn now at night—that has been topped with the stalks stacked up to dry—an inexpressibly dry rich sweet ripening scent. I feel as if I were an ear of ripening corn myself. Is not the whole air then a compound of such odors undistinguishable? (September 5, 1851 [7:73–75])

The previous passage suggests that Thoreau is painting a picture of nature's reflection on itself, of the light of the unexplored stars on the moonlight cast up from the sheeny lake. Yet the passage also corrects the notion that only vision is at stake, transferring Thoreau's attention from the vacancy which the light illuminates to a "great many particular fragrances— A field of ripening corn now at night—that has been topped off with stalks stacked up to dry—an inexpressibly dry rich sweet ripening scent"—for these envelop Thoreau and figuratively occupy the space from which visible objects have been cleared. The passage presents a series of conversions: from the debris of civilization to the sparseness of natural objects (the hushed wolves, the moose looking off, the single pine) left in its wake; from the expectation (ours if not Thoreau's) that in this light something hidden will be revealed to the way in which such an expectation is dismissed by the "inexpressibl[e] . . . scent" of ripening corn; from the idea that man possesses nature ("This is my world now") to the idea that nature possesses man, making him integral to the world he had at first tried to see. In the following passage, as in the previous one, the landscape resists the revelation it seemed about to confer:

The quail—invisible—whistles—& who attends 10 A M— The white lily has opened how could it stand these heats—it has pantingly opened—and now lies stretched out by its too-long stem on the surface of the shrunken river. The air grows more & more blue.— making pretty effects [where] one wood is seen from another though a little interval. Some pigeons here are resting in the thickest of the white pines during the heat of the day—migrating no doubt. They are unwilling to move for me. Flies buz and rain about my hat—& the dead twigs & leaves of the White pine which the choppers have left here exhale a dry & almost sickening scent. A cuccoo chuckles half throtled on a neighboring tree—& now flying into the pine scares out a pigeon which flies with its handsome tail spread dashes this side and that between the trees helplessly like a ship carrying too much sail in midst of a small creek some great amiral.—having no room to manoeuvre.— A fluttering flight.

The *mts* can scarcely be seen for the blue haze only Wachusett and the near ones. (July 21, 1851 [6:604–605])

The sharpness which inaugurates the initial observation— the attendance to the bird's whistle, the clock's precise 10 a. m.—cannot withstand the almost Faulkneresque vision of the lily, which seems to do to the perceiver what the heat has done to it. Yet the point of my observation is not the anthropo-morphism of the flower nor the naturalization of the man. It is rather the suggestion that the man is drawn into and made part of the picture he would like to attend. The finding of a focus—as in the whistle of the quail or the seeing of the lily—so absorbs or exhausts the attention of the beholder that in his concentration on the density of objects as they accumulate in his line of vision and comprise a visual clutter, the man him-self, like the cuckoo he describes, has "no room to manoeu-vre." The passage vacillates between the distinctness with which it initially describes phenomena, and the way in which they blur, in the buzz of the flies; the blue of the air; the scent of chopped wood; the cuckoo's throttling; finally, in the haze that envelops not just the mountains far away but also the foreground in which the pigeon, rhythmically flying, moves because it cannot see.

When we consider the previous two passages we would like to say that we have been regarding pictures, or pictures and their beholders, although such assertions are problematic be-cause the passages are verbal. They are nonetheless composi-tions. Thoreau had read Burke's "Of the Sublime and the Beau-tiful" in 1837, and between 1852 and 1854 he read William Gilpin's tour books of the British Isles, as well as his landscape sketches and discourses on the picturesque. As Thoreau turns away from Burke's concern with the landscape's power to gen-erate affect, so he complains that Gilpin's interest in nature is narrowly aesthetic ("I wish he would look at scenery some-times not with the eye of an artist" [IV:283]), especially taking issue with Gilpin's insistence that what is beautiful in nature cannot be made so in a picture. Thoreau is not interested in nature as a composition (as Burke and Gilpin are, albeit in different ways), but is rather interested in the composition of nature, and, in fact, hopes to replicate it. He rejects Burke because he wants to redefine what it means to see without primary reference to human affect, even as he acknowledges the interference of that affect. He rejects Gilpin because he wants to write about landscapes without aestheticizing what he is seeing, even as he acknowledges that to consider nature's composition is to make a composition of it oneself.

Many of Thoreau's pictures are therefore characterized by moments of tension between what is seen purely (civilization taken out of the landscape) and the beholder's implicit acknowledgment that vision can never be so purified. Thus in the first of the two previous Thoreau passages, the huge plane of the sheeny lake seen from the height of the cliff dominates the picture's center. Although we are told the man looks down on the lake (the lone trees behind him, the animals below) in fact we are distracted from the vertical pull implied by the depth of these gradations by the sweep ("dull whitish mark curving northward through the forest") which, crossing the picture, catches the man up in it just at the moment in which, trying to exorcise human elements, he would exit from its boundaries. The previous assertion is not only an impressionistic one, for in the conclusion of the passage we see that the ripening corn lies tangential to the light and the lake as these have been described as both central to the picture and positioned along a vertical visual axis. As the scent of the corn is what engages the man in the picture, it makes sense to say that insofar as he is a presence, his vantage may be determined not only above the light and the lake but (almost) adjacent to it. In addition, all attempts to describe the coordinates of the picture in visual terms are unbalanced by the preemptive scent of the passage's end, which overpowers its visual features.

But if the man in the passage cannot get out of the picture, hence cannot see purely (in the end, does not primarily see at all), the man in the second picture is drawn into the confusions of the picture on whose outskirts he initially stood. Thoreau's pictures often record moments when the man who would see "without civilization" is disabled from doing so. They record the moment when neutral observation catches itself in the position of having a point of view:

What can be handsomer for a picture than our river scenery now! Take this view from the firsst Conantum Cliff. First this smoothly shorne meadow on the west side of the stream, with all the swathes distinct— sprinkled with apple trees casting heavy shadows—black as ink, such as can be seen only in this clear air—this strong light—one cow wandering restlessly about in it and lowing.— Then the blue

river—scarcely darker than and not to be distinguished from the
sky—its waves driven southward or up stream by the wind—making
it appear to flow that way bordered by willows & button bushes.—
Then the narrow meadow beyond with varied lights & shades from its
waving grass which for some reason has not been cut this year.—
though so dry—now at length each grass blade bending south before
the wintery blast, as if bending for aid in that direction.— Then the
hill rising 60 feet to a terrace like plain—covered with shruboaks—
maples &c now variously tinted. (September 24, 1851 [7:142])

On the one hand what Thoreau is saying is perfectly obvious:
"If you want to see a picture of handsomeness, take this view,"
as in the colloquial "For example." Here I want to acknowledge
that what the passage has just articulated does not require that
the "example" be anything but referential of handsomeness or
of a picture, nor, in this case, that it be anything but viewed. It
does not, in itself, propose our consideration of a categorical
issue. Yet Thoreau's reiteration of the word "picture," his concern with how the contents of pictures are to be identified and
focused; with whether, if they cannot be identified, they are to
be regarded as illustrations, suggests there is in fact a categorical
issue of what examples (or what Thoreau calls "demonstra-
tions") in general are—behind this individual instance of a particular view. In this case the implication is that we are being
instructed in something we do not know: that we see objects
one at a time, as the sequence "first . . . then . . . then" illustrates; that if we are to see acutely we must segregate parts of an
apparent whole ("this smoothly shorne meadow . . . with all
the swaths distinct"); that a picture also has disparate parts (the
meadow, the river, the narrower meadow behind); that the
landscape is not a still life ("one cow wandering restlessly about
in it and lowing") which must be composed; that bringing them
perceptually together involves their interpretation (as in the perception of which way the water "appear[s] to flow" and as in the
anthropomorphic straining of the grass blades wistfully toward
summer), that the limit of a picture depends upon what we can
no longer see marked by "the hill rising 60 feet to a terrace like
plain."
    In the following passage one could again argue that Thoreau

is simply saying, "Take this prospect here, in all its glory, from moment to moment, as it passes through its moods. Wouldn't any one of those moments be a fine subject for painting as all of them together are for word painting?" Yet in the context of how many times Thoreau looks at the same view, it seems rather that he is asking, again categorically, what a picture of nature is, that he is suggesting that to know the composition of nature requires acknowledging its changes—changes that cannot be accommodated by a visual medium but rather depend upon Thoreau's own hybrid composition:

Candlelight To Conantum— The moon not quite half full. The twilight is much shorter now than a month ago, probably as the atmosphere is clearer and there is less to reflect the light. The air is cool & the ground also feels cold under my feet as if the grass were wet with dew which is not yet the case. I go through Wheelers cornfield in the twilight, where the stalks are bleached almost white—and his tops are still stacked along the edge of the field The moon is not far up above the South western horizon. Looking west at this hour the earth is an unvaried undistinguishable black in contrast with the twilight sky. It is as if you were walking in night up to your chin. There is no wind stirring. An oak tree in Hubbard's pasture stands absolutely motionless and dark against the sky. The crickets sound farther off or fainter at this season as if they had gone deeper into the sod to avoid the cold. There are no crickets heard on the alders on the causeway. The moon looks colder in the water though the waterbugs are still active. There is a great change between this and my last moon light walk— I experience a comfortable warmth when I approach the south side of a dry wood—which keeps off the cooler air. . . . The moon is too far west to be seen reflected in the river at Tupelo cliff—but the stars are reflected— The river is a dark mirror with bright points feebly fluctuating— I smell the bruised horsemint which I cannot see while I sit on the brown rocks by the shore. I see the glowworm under the damp cliff— No whippoorwills are heard tonight—and scarcely a note of any other bird. At 8 o'clock the fogs have begun which with the low half moon shining on them look like cobwebs or thin white veils spread over the earth— They are the dreams or visions of the meadow. (October 1, 1851 [7:172–174])

The passage describes a negation of aspects of the landscape as these are shown to issue from Thoreau's expectation, not from the scene. We are told about the "twilight . . . much shorter now than a month ago," with less in the atmosphere to reflect the light; about grass that feels "wet with dew which is not yet the case"; about "no wind stirring"; about "the crickets . . . fainter at this season"; "the moon . . . too far west to be seen reflected in the river"; the smell of "the bruised horsemint" Thoreau nonetheless cannot see; the whippoorwill not heard "and scarcely a note of any other bird"—this is the catalogue of phenomena displaced from the imagination. Then what would be "moving" about the picture would not be Thoreau's physical walk through the landscape but rather the mental transition from the memory of ostensibly static phenomena— the trees, the river, the light, the wind—and the transformations that seeing these phenomena again forces the mind to undergo. Saying it this way does not entirely clarify what is being transformed. The landscape? Or the mind? The mind contemplating the landscape as it was and as it is, in the double displacements of last night and a month ago, contemplating the way in which instability undercuts our conceptions. "Take this view," in both cases of Conantum, is a very different imperative when we are asked to consider it as stationary and when we are, alternatively, asked to consider its changes. If pictures of landscapes by definition undergo transformation, then we may say that although we know what it means to see, and although we know what a picture is, we do not know what it means to see a picture of a landscape, especially of a particular landscape. In Thoreau's descriptions we note the contrasts on which they are predicated—between tonight and a month ago, between this and the last moonlit walk, between the precise 10 a.m. of one of the earlier passages and the haze that immediately envelops it and any other sharp delineation.

The following passages, all written within a month and a half between November 11 and December 30, 1851, illustrate Thoreau's attempt to watch a landscape over a period of time:

A bright but cold day—finger cold— One must next wear gloves put his hands in winter quarters. There is a cold silvery light on the white pines as I go through J. P. Brown's field near Jenny Dugan's. I am glad of the shelter of the thick pine wood on the Marlboro' road—

on the plain. The roar of the wind over the pines sounds like the surf on countless beaches—an endless shore—& at intervals it sounds like a gong resounding through halls & entries.—i.e. there is a certain resounding woodliness in the tone— The sky looks mild & fair enough from this shelter—every withered blade of grass & every dry weed—as well as pine needle—reflects light— (November 11, 1851 [8:272])

As I returned through Hosmers field—the sun was setting just beneath a black cloud by which it had been obscured—and as it had been a raw & windy afternoon, its light which fell suddenly on some white pines between me & it lighting them up like a shimmering fire—and also on the oak leaves & chestnut stems was quite a circumstance. It was from the contrast between the dark and comfortless afternoon and this bright & cheerful light almost fire— The eastern hills & woods too were clothed in a still golden light. The light of the setting sun just emerged from a cloud and suddenly falling on & lighting up the needles of the white pine between you & it after a raw and louring afternoon near the beginning of winter is a memorable phenomenon. A sort of Indian summer in the day—which thus far has been denied to the year. After a cold grey day this cheering light almost warms us by its resemblance to fire. (November 22, 1851 [8:305])

This morning the ground is again covered with snow deeper than before.
In the afternoon walked to the east part of Lincoln— Saw a tree on the turnpike full of hickory nuts which had an agreeable appearance— Saw also quite a flock of the Pine Grosbeak a plump & handsome bird as big as a robin— When returning between Bear Hill & the RR. the sun had set & there was a very clear amber light in the west— & turning about we were surprised at the darkness in the east—the crescent of night—almost as if the air were thick a thick snowstorm were gathering—which as we had faced the west we were not prepared for—, yet the air was clear.
That kind of sunset which I witnessed on saturday & Sunday is perhaps peculiar to the late Autumn. The sun is unseen behind a hill—Only this bright white light like a fire falls on the trembling needles of the pine. (November 25, 1851 [8:307])

A rather cold and windy afternoon with some snow not yet melted on the ground. . . . While the squirrels hid themselves in the tree tops I sat on an oak stump by an old cellar hole and mused.

This squirrel is always an unexpectedly large animal to see frisking about. My eye wanders across the valley to the pine woods which fringe the opposite side, and in their aspect my eye finds something which addresses itself to my nature. Methinks that in my mood I was asking nature to give me a sign—I do not know exactly what it was that attracted my eye—I experienced a transient gladness at any rate at something which I saw. I am sure that my eye rested with pleasure on the White pines now reflecting a silvery light—the infinite stories of their boughs—tier above tier—a sort of basaltic structure—a crumbling precipice of pine horizontally stratified. Each pine is like a great green feather stuck in the ground. A myriad white pine boughs extend themselves horizontally one above & behind another each bearing its burden of silvery sun-light—with darker seams between them—as if it were a great crumbling piny precipice thus stratified—On this my eyes pastured while the squirrels were up the trees behind me. That at any rate it was that I got by my afternoon walk—a certain recognition from the pine. some congratulation. (November 30, 1851 [8:308])

Ah dear nature—the mere remembrance, after a short forgetfulness, of the pine woods! I come to it as a hungry man to a crust of bread. (December 12, 1851 [8:310])

The Pitch pine woods on the right of the Corner road. A piercing cold afternoon—wading in the snow—R. Rice was going to Sud. to put his bees into the cellar for fear they would freeze— He had a small hive—not enough to keep each other warm. The Pitch pines hold the snow well. It lies now in balls on their plumes—and in streaks on their branches—their low branches rising at a small angle and meeting each other.

—A certain dim religious light comes through this roof of pine leaves & snow—it is a sombre twilight—yet in some places the sun streams in—producing the strongest contrasts of light and shade.

The winter morning is the time to see the woods & shrubs in their perfection wearing their snowy & frosty dress. Even he who visits them half an hour after sunrise will have lost some of their most delicate & fleeting beauties. The trees wear their snowy burden but coarsely after mid day—& it no longer expresses the character of the tree I observed that early in the morning every pine needle was covered with a frosty sheath—but soon after sunrise it was all gone. You walk in the Pitch pine wood as under a penthouse The stems &

branches of the trees look black by contrast You wander zigzag through the aisles of the wood—where stillness & twilight reign.

Improve every opportunity to express yourself in writing as if it were your last

I do not know but a pine wood is as substantial and as memorable a fact as a friend. I am more sure to come away from it cheered than from those who come nearest to being my friends. It is unfortunate for the chopper & the walker when the cold wind comes from the same side with the sun for then he cannot find a warm recess in which to sit. It is pleasant to walk now through open & stately white pine woods. Their plumes do not hold so much snow commonly—unless where their limbs rest or are weighed down onto a neighboring tree. It is cold but still in their midst—where the snow is untracked by man—and ever & anon you see the snow dust shone on by the sun falling from their tops & as it strikes the lower limbs producing innumerable new showers. For as after a rain there is a second rain in the woods so after a light snow there is a second snow in the woods when the wind rises. The branches of the white pine are more horizontal than those of the pitch—and the white streaks of snow on them look accordingly. I perceive that the young black oaks and the red oaks too methinks still keep their leaves as well as the white. This piercing wind is so nearly from the west this afternoon that to stand at once in a sheltered and a sunny place you must seek the SSE S S E side of the woods.

What slight but important distinctions between one creature & another—what little but essential advantages one enjoys over another—I noticed this after noon a squirrels nest high in the fork of a white pine. Thither he easily ascends—but many creatures strive in vain to get at him there. The lower branches of the hemlock point down & even trail on the ground. The whole tree making a perfect canopy. (December 17, 1851 [8:320–322])

In all the woods is heard now far & near the sound of the woodchopper's axe—a twilight sound now in the night of the year—Men having come out for fuel to the forests— As if men had stolen forth in the arctic night to get fuel to keep their fires agoing. Men go to the woods now for fuel who never go there at any other time. Why should it be so pleasing to look into a thick pine wood where the sunlight streams in & gilds it? The sound of the axes far in the horizon sounds like the dropping of the eaves. Now the sun sets suddenly without a cloud—& with scarcely any redness following so pure is the atmosphere—only a faint rosy blush along the horizon. (December 19, 1851 [8:324])

2 Pm to Fair Haven Hill & plain below— Saw a large hawk circling over a pine wood below me—and screaming apparently that he might discover his prey by their flight—Travelling ever by wider circles. What a symbol of the thoughts now soaring now descending—taking larger and larger circles or smaller and smaller—It flies not directly whither it is bound but advances by circles like a courtier of the skies No such noble progress—how it comes round as with a wider sweep of thought— But the majority is in the imagination of the beholder for the bird is intent on its prey. Circling & ever circling you cannot divine which way it will incline—till perchance it dives down straight as an arrow to its mark. It rises higher above where I stand and I see with beautiful distinctness its wings against the sky—primaries & secondaries and the rich tracery of the outline of the latter? its inner wings or wing linings within the outer—like a great moth seen against the sky. A Will-o'-the wind. Following its path as it were through the vortices of the air. the poetry of motion—not as preferring one place to another but enjoying each as long as possible. Most gracefully so surveys new scenes & revisits the old. As if that hawk were made to be the symbol of my thought how bravely he came round over those parts of the wood which he had not surveyed—taking in a new segment—annexing new territories

Without heave yo! it trims its sails,— It goes about without the creaking of a block—That American Yacht of the air that never makes a tack—though it rounds the globe itself—takes in and shakes out its reefs without a flutter.—its sky scrapers all under its control—Holds up one wing as if to admire—and sweeps off this way then holds up the other & sweeps that. If there are two concentrically circling, it is such a regatta as South hampton waters never witnessed.

Flights of imagination—Coleridgean thoughts. So a man is said to soar in his thought—Ever to fresh woods & pastures new. Rises as in thought

Snow squawls pass obscuring the sun—as if blown off from a larger storm.

Since last monday the ground has covered half a foot or more with snow & the ice also before I have had a skate Hitherto we had had mostly bare and frozen ground—Red—white—green—& in the distance dark brown are the colors of the winter landscape. I view it now from the Cliffs. The red shrub oaks on the white ground of the plain beneath make a pretty scene. Most walkers are pretty effectually shut up by the snow.

I observe that they who saw down trees in the woods with a cross-cut saw carry a mat to kneel on. It is no doubt a good lesson for the woodchopper the long day alone in the woods & he gets more than his half dollar a cord.

Say the thing with which you labor—it is a waste of time for the writer to use his talents merely. Be faithful to your genius—write in the strain that interests you most— Consult not the popular taste.

The red oak leaves are even more fresh & glossy than the white.

A clump of white pines seen far westward over the shrub-oak plain which is now lit up by the setting sun a soft feathery grove with their grey stems indistinctly seen—like human beings come to their cabin door standing expectant on the edge of the plain—impress me with a mild humanity. The trees indeed have hearts. With a certain affection the sun seems to send its farewell ray far and level over the copses to them. & they silently receive it with gratitude like a group of settlers with their children. The pines impress me as human. A slight vaporous cloud floats high over them—while in the west the sun goes down apace behind glowing pines & golden clouds like mountains skirt the horizon—

Nothing stands up more free from blame in this world than a pine tree.

The dull and blundering behavior of clowns will as surely polish the writer at last as the criticism of men of thought.

It is wonderful—wonderful—the unceasing demand that Christendom makes on you—that you speak *from a moral point of view*. Though you be a babe the cry is repent—repent. The christian world will not admit that a man has a just perception of any truth—unless at the same time he cries Lord be merciful to me a sinner.

What made the hawk mount? Did you perceive the manoever? Did he fill himself with air? Before you were aware of it he had mounted by his spiral path into the heavens.

Our County is broad and rich—for here within 20 miles of Boston I can stand in a clearing in the woods and look a mile or more over the shrub oaks to the distant pine copses and horizon of uncut woods without a house or road or cultivated field in sight.

Sunset in winter from a clearing in the woods. about well meadow head They say that the Indians of the Great Basin live on the almonds of the pine. Have I not been fed by the pine for many a year?

Go out before sun-rise or stay out till sun-set. (December 20, 1851 [8:325–329])

This morning when I woke I found it snowing—the snow fine & driving almost horizontally as if it had set in for a long storm—but a little after noon it ceased snowing & began to clear up—& I set forth for a walk. The snow which we have had for the last week or 10 days has been remarkably light & dry. It is pleasant walking in the woods now when the sun is just coming out & shining on the woods freshly covered with snow—At a distance the oak woods look very venerable—a fine hale wintry aspect things wear—and the pines all snowed up even suggest comfort. Where boughs cross each other much snow is caught—which now in all woods is gradually tumbling down—By half past 3 the sun is fairly out. I go to the cliffs. There is a narrow ridge of snow a white line on the storm side of the stem of every exposed tree. I see that there is to be a fine clear sunset, & make myself a seat in the snow on the cliff to witness it. Already a few clouds are glowing like a golden sierra just above the horizon—From a low arch the clear sky has rapidly spread eastward over the whole heavens—and the sun shines serenely—and the air is still—and the spotless snow covers the fields. The snow storm is over—the clouds have departed—the sun shines serenely—the air is still—a pure & trackless white napkin covers the ground—and a fair evening is coming to conclude all—Gradually the sun sinks—the air grows more dusky & I perceive that if it were not for the light reflected from the snow it would be quite dark—The wood chopper has started for home. I can no longer distinguish the color of the red oak leaves against the snow—but they appear black. The partridges have come forth to bud on the apple trees. Now the sun has quite disappeared— but the after-glow as I may call it—apparently the reflection from the cloud beyond which the sun went down on the thick atmosphere of the horizon—is unusually bright and lasting— Long broken clouds in the horizon in the dun atmosphere—(as if the fires of day were still smoking there) hang with red & golden edging like the saddle cloths of the steeds of the sun. Now all the clouds grow black—& I give up tonight—But unexpectedly half an hour later when I look out having got home I find that the evening star is shining brightly & beneath all the west horizon is glowing red—that dun atmosphere instead of clouds reflecting the sun—and I detect just above the horizon the narrowest imaginable white sickle of the new moon. (December 23, 1851 [8:337–339])

How deceptive the size of a large pine—Still as you approach it— even within a rod or two it looks only like a reasonable stick—fit for a string piece perchance—the average size of trees one foot in diameter—big as a keg or a half barrel it may be. Fit for the sill or the beams of an old fashioned house—This you think is a generous appreciation & allowance. Not till you stand close to its foot, upon one of its swelling insteps & compare its diameter with the diameter of your own eyeballs, do you begin to discover its width. Stand by its side & see how it shuts out a hemisphere from you. Why it is as wide as a front door. What a slender arrow—a light shaft now that you stand a rod or two off—What a billista—a battering ram—a mighty vegetable monster—a cannon, near at hand!— Now set a barrel aye a hogshead beside it. You apply your measures—The foot rule seems suddenly shrunk. Your umbrella is but half as long as it was—

The pine I saw fall yesterday measured today 105 feet—& was about 94 years old—

There was one still larger lying beside it. 115 feet long—96 yrs old—4 feet diam— the longest way. The tears were streaming from the sap wood—about 20 circles—of each. pure amber or pearly tears.

Through the drizzling fog now just before the night-fall I see from the cliffs the dark cores of pine trees that rise above the level of the tree tops—and can trace a few elm tree tops where a farm house hides beneath.

Dnuded pines stand in the clearings with no old cloak to wrap about them. only the apexes of their cones entire—telling a pathetic story of the companions that clothed them. So stands a man. It is clearing around him. He has no companions on the hills—The lonely traveller looking up wonders why he was left when his companions were taken. (December 31, 1851 [8:362])

Although not cited in their entirety except for the entries from December 19th and 20th, the passages nonetheless give a sense of what it is like to read consecutively through the *Journal*. It could be argued that any quotation considers a part as a whole, but in most cases the status of the passage under consideration has been determined by a reader who will establish an argument (ostensibly supported by the text) for analyzing the passage this rather than some other way. To take a passage out of context may be to remove it from material which substantiates or contradicts it, but the very ability to evaluate these distinctions suggests that for the particular reader the idea of the subject has not *a priori* been confused by competitive ways to look at it. If we return to the first passage in the sequence, though, we see the ways in which the *Journal* makes it especially problematic to determine a focus for the subjects it presents. The passage, as I initially cited it, concluded as follows:

A bright but cold day—finger cold— One must next wear gloves put his hands in winter quarters. There is a cold silvery light on the white pines as I go through J. P. Brown's field near Jenny Dugan's. I am glad of the shelter of the thick pine wood on the Marlboro' road— on the plain. The roar of the wind over the pines sounds like the surf on countless beaches—an endless shore—& at intervals it sounds like a gong resounding through halls & entries.—i.e. there is a certain resounding woodliness in the tone— The sky looks mild & fair enough from this shelter—every withered blade of grass & every dry weed—as well as pine needle—reflects light—

Ending the quotation there emphasizes the contrasts between the sublimity of the scene (the roar of the wind, beaches which are countless, an interminable shore) and a brittle, beautiful light which shows the landscape in small (reflecting on its parts, on the needles of the pine, on "every withered blade of grass"). The quotation draws attention to the way in which two aspects of the landscape compete with each other. To cite the paragraph's end, however, turns from this contrast to Thoreau's exclusive focus on the intensity of the light:

The lately dark woods are open & light—the sun shines in upon the stems of trees which it has not shone on since spring—Around the edges of ponds the weeds are dead and there to the light penetrates—The atmosphere is less moist & gross & light is universally dispersed. We are greatly indebted to these transition seasons or states of the atmosphere—which show us thus phenomena which belong not to the summer or the winter of any climate. The brilliancy of the autumn is wonderful—this flashing brilliancy—as if the atmosphere were phosphoric.

Neither way of quoting the passage (one emphasizing contrast, the other concentration) acknowledges its context as this is redefined by the paragraphs which precede and follow it:

Living much out of doors—in the sun & wind—will no doubt produce a certain roughness of character—will cause a thicker cuticle to grow over some of the finer sensibilities of our nature as on the face hands—or as severe manual labor deprives the hands of some of the delicacy of their touch. So staying in the house on the other hand may produce a softness & smoothness not to say thinness of skin—accompanied by an increased sensibility to certain impressions.—And no doubt it is a nice matter to proportion rightly the thick & thin skins. Perhaps we should be more susceptible to some influences important to our intellectual growth—if the sun had shown & the wind blown on us a little less. As too much manual labor calluses the hand and deprives it of the exquisiteness of the touch. But then methinks that is a scurf that will fall off fast enough—that the natural remedy is to be found in the proportion which the night bears to the day—The winter to the summer &c. Thought to experience.

2 Pm

A bright but cold day—finger cold—One must next wear gloves put his hands in winter quarters. There is a cold silvery light on the white pines as I go through J. P. Brown's field near Jenny Dugan's. I am glad of the shelter of the thick pine wood on the Marlboro' road— on the plain. The roar of the wind over the pines sounds like the surf on countless beaches—an endless shore—& at intervals it sounds like a gong resounding through halls & entries.—i.e. there is a certain resounding woodliness in the tone— The sky looks mild & fair enough from this shelter—every withered blade of grass & every dry weed—as well as pine needle—reflects light—The lately dark woods are open & light—the sun shines in upon the stems of trees which it has not shone on since spring—Around the edges of ponds the weeds are dead and there to the light penetrates—The atmosphere is less moist & gross & light is universally dispersed. We are greatly indebted to these transition seasons or states of the atmosphere—which show us thus phenomena which belong not to the summer or the winter of any climate. The brilliancy of the autumn is wonderful—this flashing brilliancy—as if the atmosphere were phosphoric.

When I have been confined to my chamber for the greater part of several days by some employment or perchance by the ague—till I felt weary & houseworn—I have been conscious of a certain softness to which I am otherwise & commonly a stranger—in which the gates were loosened to some emotions— And if I were to become a confirmed invalid I see how some sympathy with mankind & society might spring up.

Yet what is my softness good for even to tears— It is not I but nature in me. I laughed at myself the other day to think that I cried while reading a pathetic story. I was no more affected in spirit than I frequently am methinks—the tears were merely a phenomenon of the bowels—& I felt that that expression of my sympathy so unusual with me was something mean—& such as I should be ashamed to have the subject of it understand. I had a cold in my head withal

about those days. I found that I had some bowels—but then it was
because my bowels were out of order. (8:271–274)

One could see the middle paragraph as an exemplification of
what precedes it. For although the "2 Pm" marks a disjunction
between the two paragraphs, although Thoreau goes outside to
see something else, going out and staying in are in fact part of
the dichotomy initially contemplated, and the "something
else" he observes illustrates the "proportion" reflected upon in
the first paragraph. In fact, the middle paragraph restates the
intial opposition—between "roughness" and "sensibility"—in
terms of the land's undifferentiated mass and a discriminating
light which individuates the mass by playing up its features. In
that same middle paragraph, however, the reiteration of contrast gives way to Thoreau's concentration on light and to light
as a concentration ("The brilliancy of the autumn is wonderful—this flashing brilliancy—as if the atmosphere were
phosphoric").

Then what is being demonstrated? The exemplification of a
subject becoming a subject in its own right? What would this
subject be? The massiveness of the landscape thrown into relief
by the light as it shows us, in opposition, the detail of grass
and pine needles? Or the light's brilliance which, bearing down
on the land, has itself become pervasive? If light *is* meant to be
a subject in its own right, why does Thoreau return to the
initial dichotomy of "roughness" and "softness"? We could say
that there is not one but rather several not entirely differentiated subjects—the particularities of the landscape in their full
autonomy and harmony, as distinct pieces of a distinct whole.
Specified in other terms, the passage shows us (1) the discrepancy *between* man's exposure to nature and his seclusion from
nature; (2) comparable discrepancies viewed *in* nature; (3) one
of nature's features (light) that, dominating the landscape, ob-
scures all contrasts; (4) a return to the ruminations about indoors and outdoors, specifically to the idea that the "softness"
of staying indoors does not issue from the self, is "not [a property of] I," but of "nature in me"—a return to the initial
dichotomy which inverts, without commenting on, its ostensibly well-delineated terms. In a mechanical context, my ques-

tions about the focus of the passage are generated by a doubt about how to quote the passage. Knowing how to quote a passage involves deciding the purpose for which you are invoking it and thereby the basis on which you determine its boundaries.

Thoreau compromises our ability to accomplish this task without seeing what we do as arbitrary. Although he first illustrates how one subject is converted into another, it is finally unclear to us which is the subject and which the illustration. (Here I mean to differentiate "subject" and "illustration" as Thoreau did in the assertion, "Talk of demonstrating the rotation of the earth on its axis, see the sun or the moon rise," where the sun's rising is an illustration of the rotation of the earth). However, as we cannot see the relation of the four concerns Thoreau takes up, we also cannot describe their focus, the hierarchical relation of their respective parts, the perspective from which the subject (man's relation to nature) is connected to its illustration in the two middle paragraphs, for the latter turns into a subject (nature's relation to itself) in its own right. If we return to the considerations Thoreau was proposing—"What is a picture?" "What is a composition?"—then the phrase "Take this view" which initially seemed obvious is precisely what is at issue. For of what passages are examples and what examples are, is—for us looking at the *Journal*, as for Thoreau looking at the landscape—what we are in doubt of.

Another way to put this is to argue that Thoreau is not randomly regarding nature day after day; rather he is collecting evidence ("field notes") for an ultimate totality (a "history of these fields") which at any given moment evades him. Despite the fact that these piecemeal observations are to be part of a whole, how each field note is to be delimited or focused is impossible to determine since no human perspective could predicate the criteria for such an assessment. Thoreau is therefore a man collecting evidence for a case he is not in a position to make because he is not in a position to know. The hope is that if he sustains the endeavor, he will have *composed* the whole picture that, at any given moment, he is unable to see. The "discipline" of the record depends upon sustaining a project in which the description of natural occurrence cannot, by definition, be "memorable," for though these phenomena are to be noted, why they are to be noted evades comprehension.

On December 25, 1851, Thoreau explicitly comments on the problem we have been considering—how to understand the focus of a subject (Thoreau here calls it a view) when we cannot determine a single or stable impression of it, and when it is moreover detached from the reason for which we contemplate it.

It would be a truer discipline for the writer to take the least film of thought that floats in the twilight sky of his mind for his theme—about which he has scarcely one idea (that would be teaching his ideas how to shoot) faintest intimations—shadowiest subjects—make a lecture on this—by assiduity and attention get perchance two views of the same—increase a little the stock of knowledge—clear a new field instead of manuring the old— Instead of making a lecture out of such obvious truths—hacknied to the minds of all thinkers— We see to soon to ally the perceptions of the mind to the experience of the hand—to prove our gossamer truths practical to show their connexion with our every day life (better show their distance from our every day life) to relate them to the cider mill and the banking institution. Ah give me pure mind—pure thought. Let me not be in haste to detect the *universal law*, let me see more clearly a particular instance of it. Much finer themes I aspire to—which will will yield no satisfaction to the vulgar mind—not one sentence for them— Perchance it may convince such that there are more things in heaven & earth than are dreamed of in their philosophy. Dissolve one nebula—& so destroy the nebular system & hypothesis. Do not seek expressions—seek thoughts to be expressed. By perseverance you get two views of the same rare truth.

That way of viewing things you know of— least insisted on by you however—least remembered—take that view—adhere to that—insist on that—see all things from that point of view— Will you let these intimations go unattended to and watch the door bell or knocker? That is your text. Do not speak for other men— Speak for yourself.— They show you as in a vision the kingdoms of this world—and of all the worlds—but you prefer to look in upon a puppet-show. Though you should only speak to one kindred mind in all time—though you should not speak to one—but only utter aloud that you may the more completely realize & live in the idea which contains the reason of your life—that you may build yourself up to the height of your conceptions—that you may remember your creator—in the days of your youth and justify his ways to man—that the end of life may not be its amusement— Speak though your thought presupposes the non existence of your hearers.—thoughts that transcend life & death. What though mortal ears are not fitted to hear absolute truth.— Thoughts that blot out the earth are best conceived in the night when darkness has already blotted it out from sight. Not in all senses level to the understandings of men

We look upward for inspiration. (8:344–346)

Liberated from the impulse to reconcile too quickly one view with another, we might arrive at "pure mind" in which we see "particular instances" which are not just discrete but contradictory as well, as an "unattended intimation" is contradictory to the clatter of the "door bell or knocker." Hence these "views" do not lead to conclusions. They are rather "examples" or illustrations detached from any coherent knowledge of what is being exemplified.

The notion that two views of the same thought (which can be drawn to no conclusions because they lead in opposite directions) "increase . . . the stock of knowledge"; that Thoreau will ally himself with that view most inimical to his mind and to its consequences in experience; that illustrations are therefore pointless, or we must resist their point, suggest that "to talk of demonstrating the rotation of the earth on its axis" and to "see the sun and moon rise" may both be imperatives of the single passage from which they come, but they are ones which, as the grammatical ellipsis indicates, fail to specify the particularities of their connection. In the absence of connection, the movement of the mind is like the sweep of the hawk in the passage from December 20, 1851, cited earlier in its entirety:

What a symbol of the thoughts now soaring now descending—taking larger and larger circles or smaller and smaller—It flies not directly whither it is bound but advances by circles like a courtier of the skies No such noble progress—how it comes round as with a wider sweep of thought— But the majority is in the imagination of the beholder for the bird is intent on its prey. (8:325)

In juxtaposing three of Thoreau's entries—the one in which examples and subjects are not easy to differentiate; the entry in which we are told we must articulate two views of the same thought; the entry in which thought is analogized to the circling of a hawk—I have implicitly suggested that for Thoreau (1) examples are subjects; (2) that to learn how to think one must discover how to embrace two views of the same thought and, having done so, leave them unreconciled (thus, for example, Thoreau disallows any single way to understand the relationship between the respective paragraphs which touch on the "proportion" between "nature" and "nature in me"); (3) that "circling" results from the evasion of conclusions; (4) that it is to the pointlessness of this circling that Thoreau aspires, and which, he maintains, takes perseverance. What these passages have in common is their evasion of connection.

In chapters two and three we considered the problem of connection in terms of Thoreau's rejection of an analogic relation between man and nature, and his rejection as well of a symbolic way of speaking of it. In the fourth chapter we considered our connection to the *Journal* as it is made contingent upon posthumous publication. In each case, the linguistic and the auditory one, relations are implied and are made discontinuous, double, or only partially apparent, as if to posit connections that are also unclarified. In the previous pages we have seen that the sabotaging of connection touches professional issues (how we are to assess the work or to determine the relation of its parts), for we have looked at passages which suggest that the avoidance of clear relation—between subjects and examples, between one part of a passage and another, between laws and their illustrations—is integral not simply to writing in a journal but to that particular journal writing which involves thinking about nature. "Circling & ever circling you cannot divine which way it will incline—till perchance it dives straight as an arrow to its mark." In the case of the *Journal* what is the mark?

We suppose "thinking" is the exploration of a delineated subject, and we presume, in addition, that successful thinking has a point, whether it be the solution of a problem or the completion of an idea. What would count as completion apparently involves finding the end of the idea. Such a conception of ideas suggests they are tasks to be worked out and left behind.

In *Walden*, in a passage from "The Beanfield" (whose origin in the *Journal* entry of December 20, 1851, will be apparent) we see how such resignation looks:

When my hoe tinkled against the stones, that music echoed to the woods and the sky, and was an accompaniment to my labor which yielded an instant and immeasurable crop. It was no longer beans that I hoed, nor I that hoed beans; and I remembered with as much pity as pride, if I remembered at all, my acquaintances who had gone to the city to attend the oratorios. The night-hawk circled over head in the sunny afternoons—for I sometimes made a day of it—like a mote in the eye, or in heaven's eye, falling from time to time with a swoop and a sound as if the heavens were rent, torn at last to very rags and tatters, and yet a seamless cope remained; small imps that fill the air and lay their eggs on the ground on bare sand or rocks on the tops of hills, where few have found them; graceful and slender like ripples caught up from the pond, as leaves are raised by the wind to float in the heavens; such kindredship is in Nature. The hawk is aerial brother of the wave which he sails over and surveys, those his perfect air-inflated wings answering to the elemental unfledged pinions of the sea. Or sometimes I watched a pair of hen-hawks circling high in sky, alternately soaring and descending, approaching and leaving one another, as if they were the embodiment of my own thoughts. (*W*, 159)

We are later told that the hoeing of beans does not exist for its own sake but rather exists "for the sake of tropes and expression, to serve a parable-maker one day" (*W*, 162). Insofar as the hawk's motion is enlisted in the parable, it (and the thought of which it is an emblem) is assigned a task—to connect heaven and earth. Thus we are told that the hawk's motion is like a "mote in the eye, or in heaven's eye," as if in the mesmeric rhythm of the bird's (or thought's) "soaring and descending" the two become first disjunctive, as the "or" implies, then coordinate, proving kindredship in Nature, then utterly confused ("It was no longer beans that I hoed, nor I that hoed beans"). Although it is true that the first hawk as "mote in the eye" does not express the subjectivity that the two hen-hawks ("the embodiment of my own thoughts") later do, it does connect the earth on which man stands with the heavens in which the bird flies, initiating a conflation which the hen-hawks will complete. In the expropriation of nature by cerebral intention Thoreau seems to suggest that the hawk exists—thought exists—to accomplish a connection Thoreau himself calls "seamless." In passages like this one, subjects in *Walden* are closed to our consideration and we stand on one side of them or the other. Either we are already in possession of what Thoreau wants to say—or we are outside of it, asked to take on faith what we are prohibited from contemplating. Thinking our way into the issues raised by Thoreau is the option of which *Walden* deprives us. For thought in the book exists as a figure of speech, as a trope for connections whose meaning is predetermined. If the problem in *Walden* is that thought is a dead end because we have no access to it, the problem in the *Journal* is that thinking is endless.

The *Journal* is the record of a man thinking about nature, however at odds with each other these thoughts or views might be. One could of course notice narrative connections within single *Journal* volumes, and so integrate the entries by implying their sequence develops observations not in fact discrete. (Here when I use the word "volume," I refer to the author's manuscript volumes. I thus distinguish them from the volumes of the 1906 edition, which are arbitrary with respect to Thoreau's numbering system.) One might, for example, describe the structure of the seventh manuscript volume (August 21 to October 7, 1851) as one which begins by talk about artistry, specifically about the artistry which can reproduce the landscape, and which concludes with a trip to Fair Haven Pond, converting talk about painting the landscape to painting by "talk" the variations of moonlight, firelight, light through the mist, as each is reflected in the water. Similarly, one could thematize the sixth volume (July 8 to August 20, 1851) by suggesting it converts a literal trip from Boston to Concord to a series of meditations on what it means to be a traveller:

> Coming out of town—willingly as usual—when I saw that reach of Charles River just above the Depot—the fair still water this cloudy evening suggesting the way to eternal peace & beauty—whence it

flows—the placid lake-like fresh water so unlike the salt brine—
affected me not a little— I was reminded of the way in which Wordsworth so coldly speaks of some natural visions or scenes "giving him
pleasure". This is perhaps the first vision of elysium on this [rout]
from Boston. . . . What can be more impressive than to look up a
noble river just at evening—one perchance which you have never
explored—& behold its placid waters reflecting the woods—& sky
lapsing inaudibly toward the ocean—to behold as a lake—but know it
as a river—tempting the beholder to explore it—& his own destiny. at
once. haunt of waterfowl—this was above the factories—all that I saw
That water could never have flowed under a factory—how *then* could
it have reflected the sky? (July 9, 1851 [6:555–556])

As this volume of the *Journal* is in fact a sustained meditation
on heat, on moonlight, on the peculiarities of summer, on the
science of perceiving these—hence on Darwin and Linnaeus
("Is it to be kept up long this habit of close observation?" and
on June 15, 1851: "Darwin still" [5:505]), we see the journey
delivers Thoreau from a place to a season regarded in its
prime, for going out of town is like going into summer for the
first time regarded. Our impulse to view the volume as the
story of a voyage is sanctioned by its last sentence: "A traveller
who looks at things with an impartial eye may see what the
oldest inhabitant has not observed" (August 20, 1851 [6:714]),
and is anticipated by a sentence from an entry written a month
before: "There would be [this] advantage in travelling in your
own country . . . that you would be so thoroughly prepared to
understand what you saw—" (June 12, 1851 [5:488]). Hence
Thoreau will note the decline of the moon from one night to
the next, concluding, "You have lost some light, it is true, but
you have got this simple & magnificent stillness, brooding like
genius" (July 12, 1851 [6:567]). Such descriptions suggest that a
travelogue and transport are as inseparable as the aimless
walking which characterizes the volume is inseparable from
moments of transfixed attention to objects—in this case, the
moonlight—which periodically interrupt it.

In other volumes the proximity of subjects makes them seem
connected. Thus in the eighth volume (October 7, 1851 to January 11, 1852) questions about how man is to see nature, how to
write about what he sees, how to preserve what he has writ-

ten, how to regard it, and how landscapes are elucidated by different slants of light, intersect, suggesting that nature's illumination by light and by human perception are integral. Thus in manuscript volumes 15 and 16 (especially between March and November 1853), where the questions of what things shall be called occupies Thoreau's attention, the *Journal* specifies a relationship between "naming" and "timing," for designation is seen to depend upon how a phenomenon's first appearance can be distinguished from one year to another.

Yet thematizing the volumes thus (suggesting, for example, that one is about talk of painting the landscape and its actualization in talk; another about the conjunction of disparate attitudes toward science; a third about the intersection of travelogue and transport; a fourth about the adjacency of light and perception; a fifth about the contingency of designation and timing), while not falsifying what is in the volumes, fails to explain the way in which what we read makes such connections seem trivial, for we are continually asked to see that the totality of perception lies not in unifying thematic descriptions, but in single phenomena and in the compilation of single descriptions of those phenomena. Moreover, as the *Journal* progresses, it becomes less hospitable to our procedures of such characterization or excerption, for, as I have been noting, it refuses to clarify how subjects and examples are related to each other. Our inability to excerpt *Journal* passages from the later years, especially passages which have a literary finish, as, for instance, the passages in *Walden* do, has led us falsely to conclude that after 1854 Thoreau's interest in nature waned (hence the customary interpretation of Thoreau's invigorated dedication to detail after the publication of *Walden*).

Thoreau himself belies this simplification. While on August 19, 1851, he will complain, "I fear that the character of my knowledge is from year to year becoming more distinct & scientific— That in exchange for views as wide as heaven's cope I am being narrowed down to the field of the microscope" (6:708), the next day he will correct himself, acknowledging the value of the scientific: "Botany is worth studying if only for the precision of its terms—to learn the value of words & of system. It is wonderful how much pains has been taken to describe a flowers leaf—, compared [for] instance with the care that is taken in describing a psychological fact" (6:711)—his suspicion of science and his passion for it attendant upon each other. It is thus untrue that scientific descriptions of nature and perceptual descriptions of it (which the former are presumed to preempt) are incompatible. Thoreau had explicitly written: "I have a commonplace book for facts and another for poetry, but I find it difficult always to preserve the vague distinction which I had in mind, for the most interesting and beautiful facts are so much the more poetry, and that is their success" (February 18, 1851 [9:544]).[39] In the most violent swing away from the traditional characterization of Thoreau's position in the later *Journal* years (a man of science lamenting the dryness of scientific inclinations), on July 18, 1852, Thoreau insists: "Every poet has trembled on the verge of science" (IV:239); that is, poetry must achieve the precision of science, the poet must emulate the "natural philosopher." This aspiration is fulfilled in the final volumes, whose arduous investigations are a testament to the very passion Thoreau has ostensibly declined to feel. To read these final volumes is to be struck by the inseparability of detail and devotion, not as it is inevitable but as Thoreau has made it so. Many years earlier, Thoreau had written in another context, "Do not all strange sounds thrill us as *human* till we have learned to refer them to their proper source?" (September 4, 1854 [VII: 12]). In the later volumes, especially twenty-four through twenty-six (the 1906 volume X dating from August 1857 to June 1858), which offer particularly cogent examples of how light and color may be discerned and described, excitement is generated by the discovery of proper reference.

Focusing on the characteristics of two glowworms, Thoreau writes on August 8, 1857:

Examining them by night, they are about three quarters of an inch long as they crawl. Looking down on *one*, it shows two bright dots near together on the head, and, along the body, nine transverse lines of light, succeeded by two more bright dots at the other extremity, wider apart than the first. There is also a bright dot on each side opposite the transverse lines. It is a greenish light, growing more green as the worm is brought into more light. A slumbering, glowing, *inward* light, as if shining for itself inward as much as outward. The other worm, which was at first curled up still and emitted a duller light, was one and one twentieth inches in length and also showed two dots of light only on the forward segment. When stretched out, as you look down on them, they have a square-edged look, like a row of buns joined together. Such is the ocular illusion. But whether stretched out or curled up, they look like some kind of rare and precious gem, so regularly marked, far more beautiful than a uniform mass of light would be. (X:3–4])

A month later (September 18, 1857), still preoccupied by these considerations, Thoreau records in his *Journal*:

Coming home through the street in a thunder-shower at ten o'clock this night, it was exceedingly dark. . . . When the lightning lit up the street, almost as plain as day, I saw that it was the same *green* light that the glow-worm emits. Has the moisture something to do with it in both cases? (X:36)

Such questions probe a given experience, revealing its texture as finely and as fully as earlier entries:

Tell me precisely the value and significance of these transient gleams which come sometimes at the end of the day, before the close of the storm, final dispersion of the clouds, too late to be of any service to the works of man for the day, and notwithstanding the whole night after may be overcast! Is not this a language to be heard and understood? There is, in the brown and grey earth and rocks, and the withered leaves and bare twigs at this season, a purity more corre- spondent to the light itself than summer offers. (October 28, 1857 [X:134])

Two last examples from March 18, 1858, emphasize the way in which ecstasy is inseparable from calculation of the physical— from the noting of intervals in the first case:

Every third tree is lit with the most subdued but clear ethereal light, as if it were the most delicate frostwork in a winter morning, reflecting no heat, but only light. And as they rock and wave in the strong wind, even a mile off, the light courses up and down there as over a field of grain; *i.e.*, they are alternately light and dark, like looms above the forest, when the shuttle is thrown between the light woof and the dark web, weaving a light article,—spring goods for Nature to wear. At sight of this my spirit is like a lit tree. (X:305–306)

and from the act of simple addition, in the second, in which something at which we had repetitively looked and never seen before obstructs our line of vision:

After walking for a couple of hours the other day through the woods, I came to the base of a tall aspen, which I do not remember to have seen before, standing in the midst of the woods in the next town, still thickly leaved and turned to greenish yellow. It is perhaps the largest of its species that I know. It was by merest accident that I stumbled on it, and if I had been sent to find it, I should have thought it to be, as we say, like looking for a needle in a haymow. All summer, and it chances for so many years, it has been concealed to me; but now, walking in a different direction, to the same hilltop from which I saw the scarlet oaks, and looking off just before sunset, when all other trees visible for miles around are reddish or green, I distinguish my new acquaintance by its yellowish color. Such is its fame, at last, and reward for living in that solitude and obscurity. It is the most distinct tree in all the landscape, and would be the cynosure of all eyes here. Thus it plays its part in the choir. . . . It seemed the obscurest of trees. Now it was seen to be equally peculiar for its distinctness and prominence. (October 31, 1858 [XI:268])

What the *Journal* substitutes for plot or thematic coherence is occurrences like the following:

As I returned through Hosmers field—the sun was setting just beneath a black cloud by which it had been obscured—and as it had been a raw & windy afternoon, its light which fell suddenly on some white pines between me & it lighting them up like a shimmering fire—and also on the oak leaves & chestnut stems was quite a circumstance. (November 22, 1851 [8:305])

Some years later, in 1942, Wallace Stevens, who gives Thoreau passing mention in a single letter, charting his own course of particulars, would write *Notes toward a Supreme Fiction*, whose concerns seem a ghostly echo of what we have been reading:

From this the poem springs: that we live in a place
That is not our own and, much more, not ourselves.

Thoreau had himself repeatedly equated the keeping of a *Journal* with the work of a poet. I want, in fact, to suggest Thoreau's word is a considered one, and to ask how the three headings to Stevens's *Notes toward a Supreme Fiction* (which tell us prescriptively what poems are to do) illuminate what we have been considering: "It must be abstract. It must change. It must give pleasure." It is easy to see how Thoreau's *Journal* adheres to the last of these requirements, gives pleasure and changes; the *Journal* records the pleasure of change (Stevens would call it "the pleasure of merely circulating"). But Thoreau's attention to the phenomenal objects and his rejection of the representative (in the form of emblems and names) notwithstanding, what most characterizes Thoreau's *Journal* and makes it almost unreadable is its fantastic adherence to, its phantasmal anticipation of, Steven's first prescriptive statement: "It must be abstract." For the premise behind Thoreau's writing of the *Journal* lies in the brazen belief that interest is generated by the very act of observing contrasts, disassociated from story, progression, from anything at all. Contrast may be revealed in seeing a phenomenon from one year to the next. It may be revealed in double visions of the same phenomenon. Or, translated into spatial terms, it may be illuminated by the trees which create a background for it, when "the sun . . . setting just behind a black cloud by which it had been obscured" returns and turns into light "which fell suddenly on some white pines between me & it lighting them up like a shimmering fire," making what Thoreau calls "quite a circumstance." Contrast *is* the circumstance that is illuminated by those trees, for what Thoreau loves about nature is its endless repetitions as the man in the *Journal* will learn to differentiate them, will make perception ape the versatility of the seasons: "It was summer, and now again it is winter. Nature loves this rhyme so well that she never tires of repeating it. . . . What a poem! an epic in blank verse. . . . It is solid beauty" (December 7, 1856 [IX:168]).

What the passages in Thoreau's *Journal* at which we have

been looking have in common is an interest in relations which seem devoid of content, or whose content could be specified as man's pleasure in his ability to negotiate the continuously reiterated terms of likeness and change. How but as an interest in contrast are we to understand the fascination at the divided light of the glowworm, or the pleasure in the discovery that lightning and the glowworm exhibit the same green source of light, or the mathematical assessment that every third tree is lit with ethereal light, or the discovery of addition inherent in the experience that the aspen always before Thoreau's eyes he suddenly *sees?* Whether nature is of interest because it expresses relations purified of content, or whether interest in relations made abstract (because they have no analogic meaning outside our perception of them) is prompted by observing nature purely is impossible to decipher, and that distinction fails to matter. The accomplishment of the work is the astonishing ability to sustain, to be mesmerized by the changes of nature over so many years, as in the following entry, on July 4, 1852, Thoreau will delimit them in twenty-four hours:

July 4. *Sunday*. 3 A.M.—To Conantum, to see the lilies open.
I hear an occasional crowing of cocks in distant barns, as has been their habit for how many thousand years. It was so when I was young; and it will be so when I am old. I hear the croak of a tree-toad as I am crossing the yard. I am surprised to find the dawn so far advanced. There is a yellowish segment of light in the east, paling a star and adding sensibly to the light of the waning and now declining moon. There is very little dew on the uplands. I hear a little twittering and some clear singing from the seringo and the song sparrow as I go along the back road, and now and then the note of a bullfrog from the river. The light in the east has acquired a reddish tinge near the horizon. Small wisps of cloud are already fuscous and dark, seen against the light, as in the west at evening. It being Sunday morning, I hear no early stirring farmer driving over a bridge. The crickets are not remarkably loud at this season. The sound of a whip-poor-will is wafted from the woods. Now, on the Corner road, the hedges are alive with twittering sparrows, a bluebird or two, etc. The daylight now balances the moonlight. How short the nights! The last traces of day have not disappeared much before 10 o'clock, or perchance 9.30, and before 3 A. M. you see them again in the east,—probably 2.30,—

leaving about five hours of solid night, the sun so soon coming round again. The robins sing, but not so loud and long as in the spring. I have not been awakened by them latterly in the mornings. Is it my fault? Ah! those mornings when you are awakened in the dawn by the singing, the matins, of the birds! I hear the dumping sound of frogs now on the causeway. Some small clouds in the east are reddish fuscous. There is no fog on the river nor in the meadows. The king-bird twitters (?) on the black willows. Methinks I saw the not yet extinguished lights of one or two fireflies in the darker ruts in the grass, in Conant's meadow. The moon yields to the sun. She pales even in the presence of his *dawn*. It is chiefly the spring birds that I hear at this hour, and in each dawn the spring is thus revived. The notes of the sparrows and the bluebirds and the robin have a promi-nence now which they have not by day.

The light is more and more general, and some low bars begin to look bluish as well as reddish. (Elsewhere the sky wholly clear of clouds.) The dawn is at this stage far lighter than the brightest moon-light. I write by it. Yet the sun will not rise for some time. Those bars are reddening more above one spot. They grow purplish, or lilac rather. White and whiter grows the light in the eastern sky. (And now, descending to the Cliff by the riverside, I cannot see the low horizon and its phenomena.) I love to go through these old apple orchards so irregularly set out. Sometimes two trees standing close together. The rows of grafted fruit will never tempt me to wander amid them like these. A bittern leaves the shore at my approach. I suppose it is he whose excrement has whitened the rocks, as if a mason had spilled his whitewash. A nighthawk squeaks and booms, before sunrise. The insects shaped like shad-flies (some which I see are larger and yellowish) begin to leave their cases (and selves?) on the stems of the grasses and the rushes in the water. I find them so weak they can hardly hold on. I hear the blackbird's *conqueree,* and the kingfisher darts away with his alarum and outstretched neck. Every lily is shut.

Sunrise. I see it gilding the top of the hill behind me, but the sun itself is concealed by the hills and woods on the east shore. A very slight fog begins to rise now in one place on the river. There is something serenely glorious and memorable to me in the sight of the first cool sunlight now gilding the eastern extremity of the bushy island in Fair Haven, that wild lake. The subdued light and the repose remind me of Hades. In such sunlight there is no fever. It is such an innocent pale yellow as the spring flowers. It is the pollen of the sun, fertilizing plants. The color of the earliest spring flowers is as cool and innocent as the first rays of the sun in the morning falling on woods and hills. The fog not only rises upward (about two feet), but at once there is a motion from the sun over the surface. What means this endless motion of water-bugs collected in little groups on the surface and ceaselessly circling about their centre, as if they were a family hatched from the eggs on the under side of a pad? Is not this motion intended partly to balk the fishes? Methinks they did not begin to move till sunrise. Where were they? And now I see an army of skaters advancing in loose array,—of chasseurs or scouts, as Indian allies are drawn in old books.

Now the rays of the sun have reached my seat, a few feet above the water; flies begin to buzz, mosquitoes to be less troublesome. A hummingbird hums by over the pads up the river, as if looking, like myself, to see if lilies have blossomed. The birds begin to sing generally, and, if not loudest, at least most noticeably on account of the quietness of the hour, just before—a few minutes before—sunrise. They do not sing so incessantly and earnestly, as a regular thing, half an hour later.

Carefully looking both up and down the river, I could perceive that the lilies began to open about fifteen minutes after the sun from over the opposite bank fell on them, which was perhaps three quarters of an hour after sunrise (which is about 4.30), and one was fully expanded about twenty minutes later. When I returned over the bridge about 6.15, there were perhaps a dozen open ones in sight. It was very difficult to find one not injured by insects. Even the buds which were just about to expand were frequently bored quite through, and the water had rotted them. You must be on hand early to anticipate insects.

One thimble-berry which will be quite ripe by to-morrow. Indigo almost expanded. I perceive the meadow fragrance on the causeway. Bobolinks still.

I bring home a dozen *perfect* lily buds,—all I can find within many rods,—which have never yet opened; I prepare a large pan of water; I cut their stems quite short; I turn back their calyx-leaves with my fingers, so that they may float upright; I touch the points of their petals, and breathe or blow on them, and toss them in. They spring open rapidly, or gradually expand in the course of an hour,—all but one or two.

At 12.30 P. M., I perceive that the lilies in the river have begun to shut up. The water has gone down so much that I can stand on the shore and pluck as many as I want, and they are the fairest ones, concealed by the pickerel-weed, often the whole plant high and dry. I go again to the river at 2.30 P. M., and every lily is shut.

I will here tell the history of my rosaceous lilies plucked the 1st of July. They were buds at the bottom of a pitcher of water all the 2d, having been kept in my hat part of the day before. On the morning of the 3d I assisted their opening, and put them in water, as I have described; but they did not shut up at noon, like those in the river, but at dark, their petals, at least, quite tight and close. They all opened again in the course of the forenoon of the 4th, but had not shut up at 10 o'clock P. M., though I found them shut in the morning of the 5th. May it be that they can bear only a certain amount of light, and these, being in the shade, remained open longer? (I think not, for they shut up in the river that quite cloudy day, July 1st.) Or is their vitality too little to permit [them] to perform their regular functions?

Can that meadow fragrance come from the purple summits of the eupatorium?

I looked down on the river behind Dodd's at 2.30 P. M., a slate-colored stream with a scarcely perceptible current, with a male and female shore; the former, more abrupt, of button-bushes and willows, the other, flat, of grass and pickerel weed alone. Beyond the former, the water being deep, extends a border or fringe of green and purplish pads lying perfectly flat on the surface, but on the latter side the pads extend a half a rood or a rod beyond the pickerel-weed,—shining pads reflecting the light, dotted with white or yellow lilies. This sort of ruff does the river wear, and so the land is graduated off to water. A tender place in Nature, an exposed vein, and Nature making a feint to bridge it quite over with a paddy film, with red-winged blackbirds liquidly warbling and whistling on the willows, and kingbirds on the elms and oaks; these pads, if there is any wind, rippling with the water and helping to smooth and allay it. It looks tender and exposed, as if it were naturally subterranean, and now, with these shields of pads, held scale-like by long threads from the bottom, she makes a feint to bridge it. So floats the Musketaquid over its segment of the sphere.

Methinks there is not even a lily, white or yellow, in Walden.

I see perfectly formed pouts by the shore of the river, one inch long. The great spatterdock lily is a rich yellow at a little distance, and, seen lying on its great pads, it is an indispensable evidence of the fertility of the river. The gratiola begins to yellow the mud by the riverside. The *Lysimachia lanceolata* var. *hybrida* is out, in the meadows. The *Rosa nitida* (?) appears to be now out of bloom. (IV:179–85)

Thoreau is documenting the opening of the lilies—those which open at home versus those which open by the river and the timing of each flower's unfolding; the lilies' sensitivity to light so they can bear only a certain amount of it; the minute attention to light (of the dawn, of the fireflies, of the brevity of "solid night" interrupted as this is by bars of color in the sky); discriminations among kinds of light (the "first cool sunlight" in which "there is no fever"; light which strengthens and climbs a few feet above water; the sun mirrored in the shining pads reflecting the light, "dotted with white or yellow lilies"); the way in which the lily pads create the illusion that the water is only surface ("these pads, if there is any wind, rippling with the water and helping to smooth and allay it") and alternatively reveal that the water has depth (for "these shields of pads" are held "scale-like by long threads from the bottom"). One thing that is not being documented is the aesthetic qualities of the scene—an assertion we could apply to the *Journal* as a whole. For an interest in aesthetics is an interest in the discernment of what is beautiful, and according to what criteria. It is an interest that cultivates judgments and principles, as, for example, *Walden* does, whereas in the *Journal*, beauty in the landscape seems always inadvertent. Although words like "prettiness" and "handsomeness" appear in the *Journal*'s passages, twenty-four years of exacting descriptions all but redefine these diminutive epithets overcome by the massive act of seeing into which they are absorbed.

In entries like the previous one, Thoreau thwarts our conventional interests and our conventional ways of understanding the idea of interest. Hence Thoreau's concern that thus far no man's life has been rich enough to be journalized, and the rectification of the poverty—the finding of sufficient richness—by taking man out of his life, or taking life out of the man, so as to bequeath it to nature. When Thoreau speaks of "sentences which are expensive toward which so many volumes—so much life went" we may suppose what is being sacrificed is the human world. The man emptied of himself and of the world of human selves, becomes "the scribe of all nature . . . the corn & the grass & the atmosphere writing." He is not exactly indistinguishable from the nature that enthralls him, but he is, as Stevens would say, "less and less human," a "savage spirit." In this spirit, on December 12, 1851, Thoreau's own words attest: "I wished to live ah! as far away as a man can think" (8:311) (exploiting the doubleness of "as far away as anyone can imagine" and the more primary "as far away as the mind can get"). There on the margin of the human and the natural Thoreau's "Book of the seasons" may not only be about nature, it may also be of it.

> After a still winter night I awoke with the impression that some question had been put to me, which I had been endeavoring in vain to answer in my sleep, as what—how—when—where? But there was dawning Nature, in whom all creatures live, looking in at my broad windows with serene and satisfied face, and no question on *her* lips. I awoke to an answered question, to Nature and daylight. The snow lying deep on the earth dotted with young pines, and the very slope of the hill on which my house is placed, seemed to say, Forward! Nature puts no question and answers none we mortals ask. (*W*, 282)

Thus begins the first paragraph of "The Pond in Winter," that chapter in which, having banished the human world, Thoreau fights a losing battle to keep from personifying the natural one, for the chapter concludes by equating nature's reason for being with our ability to ascribe significance to it: "I am thankful that this pond was made deep and pure for a symbol. While men believe in the infinite some ponds will be thought to be bottomless" (*W*, 287). The question momentarily stalled in *Walden* ("what—how—when—where") is not absent in the *Journal*; it is simply ungratified. In fact we are always conscious of the question, as of a thought half-suppressed, which might be specified as follows: What is nature's connection to the man who observes it (who sees the intervals between "myself—a pine tree & the moon nearly equidistant" or who notes the contrast of the sun behind a hill and "this bright white light [which] like a fire falls on the trembling pine needles)? What is the unspecified connection between the particular moments at which Thoreau sees the opening of the lilies and what in fact he sees? In view of this question and ones which attend it—why are we forced to observe, privileged to observe, what we have not a prayer of comprehending?—we see how some of Thoreau's assertions ("The pines impress me as human . . . The trees indeed have hearts") promise us an answer, take the form of an answer, and fail to deliver it. Although both assertions say that nature is dear because nature is human, or is like the human, in the context of the *Journal* which eschews anthropomorphism as adamantly as a work can, such assertions simply have to do with the fact the trees evoke feeling, not that they have it.

Walden accounts for our feeling for nature by suggesting that nature realizes our beliefs, externalizes them so we may see them ("While men believe in the infinite some ponds will be thought to be bottomless"). The *Journal* accounts for our feeling for nature by suggesting that nature replaces beliefs with *alternative* pictures:

> It would be worth the while to tell why a swamp pleases us.—what kinds please us—also what weather &c &c analyse our impressions. Why the moaning of the storm gives me pleasure. Methinks it is because it puts to rout the trivialness of our fairweather life & gives it at least a tragic interest. (March 31, 1852 [10:638])

To put this in the terms to which I alluded earlier, the *Journal* accounts for our feeling for nature by suggesting that the love of the lily or of the pine is generated by the fact that these natural phenomena illustrate relations in and of themselves: the crossing of the pine boughs in which "much snow is caught," the limbs of the pines frozen into place because weighted down by snow and the disruption of this stasis by "innumerable new showers . . . when the wind rises," "the infinite stories" of "pine horizontally stratified," the sight of which confers not meaning ("in my mood I was asking nature to give me a sign") but rather "a transient gladness," the "deceptive . . . size of a large pine" which, far away, looks like nothing but a "stick" but when you "stand close to its foot . . . & compare its diameter with the diameter of your own eyeballs" you see "how it shuts out a hemisphere from you" ("You apply your measures—The foot rule seems suddenly shrunk").

It is true of the whole *Journal* that when we apply our measures the rule seems suddenly shrunk, for the context of the numerous illustrations is always subordinate to a calculus of relations, which seems in and of itself to have meaning. To

inquire why such relations—such contrasts and conjunctions—
should be of interest is implicitly to ask why any particle of
experience should incite philosophical concern. To ask about
these conjunctions is to ask how the mind sees nature, how it
differentiates nature from its own mental operations, how it
invents a language for that differentiation, as, for example,
"talk" and "illustration" constitute such a language. In the
Journal, pictures of nature reveal the way in which conceptions
of nature accompany each other, or succeed each other, or are
integral to each other. The pictures exemplify conjunctions of
nature with human nature, a tree against other trees, science
and poetry, two views of the same thing. These "two views"
are not simply pictures of nature (as in the passage which
begins "Take this view" and proceeds to offer a visual composition of a landscape), they are also assertions about how views
are to be taken—about whether they are "given" or whether
they are to be sought ("that would be teaching . . . ideas how
to shoot"), and, if they are sought—if they are created—
whether by science or poetry. In alternatively advancing the
precision of science and the intuition of poetry, Thoreau asks:
If we do not anthropomorphize nature—isolate or excerpt it for
a purpose, see it in our own image or see its image in ourselves—then is it meaningless?

The text of the *Journal*—the story it tells—is that views are
double. Thoreau lives in nature's midst and theorizes about
where he lives. He measures phenomena with scientific accuracy, and alternatively, with unaided perception, intuits what
he sees. He regards the difference between nature and human
nature (makes man part of the picture he simultaneously observes) and distinguishes one part of nature from another part
of nature (removes man from the picture as if so doing he
could objectify the composition). He records nature as if to
remember it, and also suggests that as what is crucial in nature
is not in fact memorable, the reason to record it is not to recall
it but to establish a relation to it, with record and relation
synonymous with each other. He writes descriptions of nature
that amount to pictures of propositions, and suggests that
thoughts about nature, as they generate these pictures, are
inseparable from them. Descriptions *are* thoughts; to describe is

to think, is what Thoreau calls "pure mind," for as the mind has been cleared of the preconceptions which occupy it, it can receive mental pictures, can form mental pictures of the nature that it sees. This way of describing what "thinking" is makes sense of the idioms "to call a thought to mind" and to "reflect" on a thought. It reminds us of thinking as searching for something not yet there, of the foreignness of the enterprise, not of its familiarity—differentiating consciousness, which is passive, from thinking, which is not. He likens his interest in nature to a mythology of it, but his descriptions of nature, and the project as a whole, in its relentless discontinuousness, is an *anti*-mythology.

Yet to speak of the *Journal*'s conjoining of oppositions, even to see such conjunctions as dependent upon continuous observation—on perception that does not regard meaning as static but rather conceives it as endlessly undetermined (hence the *Journal* appears to have no structure, no progress, and no discrete end, for it charts the evolution of points of view inconclusive by definition)—is still to speak in terms that minimize and so miss the achievement of this work. Even if Thoreau and not his illness had put an end to the *Journal*, that fact would support my contention that Thoreau conceived a posthumous audience for this work, but it would in no way alter the shapelessness I have described, for in the context of the whole, and according to its dictum, any terminus is arbitrary.

The consequence of the doubleness and of the displacement of human perspective as I have been describing them are (1) a form of analogy which seems unfamiliar to us, for through it the mind becomes the receptacle for material that is alien to it; (2) an entire book predicated on such analogies in which the terms of the ordinary hierarchy that subordinates nature to human nature (and the ordinary way of bridging the difference between the two, by likening nature to the mind) are suspended and transposed. If the word "catechresis" could be metaphorized so it described not simply a figure of speech in which a word violates a context by its unconventional habitation there (as pictures of nature violate our conception of what should inhabit the construct we call "mind") but could also apply to forty-seven manuscript volumes (to the fact of those volumes as well as to their content) it would appropriately designate the transpositions about which I am speaking. In Thoreau's *Journal* nature and the mind are *not* like each other, or if they are, it is because man has been naturalized, because nature has been as if driven into the mind. Descriptions of nature at once displace our idea of what thoughts are, and, as these pictures exist instead of thoughts, in that replacement, seem inseparable from them, very much as subjects and examples have been made inseparable.

"Not I," Thoreau had written, "but nature in me." The *Journal* is the document that makes sense of that internalization. The internalization is not the result of analogic correspondence conventionally understood, for analogy demands for comparative purposes the existence of the very human properties driven out of this man and this work. Analogies cannot effect comparisons between nature and human nature (the two are incomparable); they must rather effect transfers, in the express sense of moving natural phenomena—or pictures of natural phenomena—into the mind and onto the page, where the mind can testify from close up to the fundamental difference between itself and what it contemplates. Hence in the *Journal* analogies do not exist to make connections; they rather exist to enact displacements, as in the following passage:

> The distant view of the open flooded Sudbury meadows, all dark blue, surrounded by a landscape of white snow, gave an impulse to the dormant sap in my veins. (March 8, 1853 [V:11])

When the life of the flooded meadows is glimpsed by the man, the act of seeing it is tantamount to internalizing it, with the integral and the alien equally insisted upon and ultimately inseparable. On July 14, 1854, Thoreau will make just such a connection: "My thoughts are driven inward, even as clouds and trees are reflected in the still, smooth water. There is an inwardness even in the mosquitoes' hum, while I am picking blueberries in the dank wood" (VI:395). In another passage and of another season: "Winter with its *inwardness* is upon us" (October 27, 1851 [8:242]). Inwardness is not so much a quality of nature as it is a way of describing how man thinks of nature: "He must all but see it." To see nature—whether the flooded Sudbury meadows, or the swamp, or winter, or the mosquitoes' humming—is to take it into the mind while all the time recognizing it is not of the mind. Such analogies present us with pictures of a man who notes natural relations outside himself, notes "a tree seen against other trees" versus "a tree seen against the sky." (In this case, "objectivity" is not being claimed for the externality that is regarded, for man creates the picture outside of which he stands.) They present us with pictures of a man who notes nature inside himself, notes "not I but nature in me" (with the strangeness of what is being regarded unmitigated by the internalization). Thus the *Journal* enacts a series of substitutions: of pictures for thoughts; of particularities for laws; of business in the woods for business in the world; of man's vision for his will; of nature that replaces the self which is given up; of illustrations for any coherent sense of what is being illustrated. Another way to put this is to say that the *Journal* redefines the personal so that it comes to mean man's involvement in nature, or his involvement with nature—we do not know what preposition to employ because we do not comprehend the relationship the preposition specifies. Hence we call the *Journal* "draft material," meaning it is preliminary. "Preliminary to what?" is a question whose implication about further retreat from the human ought to scare us sufficiently to see this work as the limit of, not the preparation for, how far a man can go. We recall Thoreau had said: "I wished to live as far away as a man can think."

I have previously asserted that the *Journal* records relations without content. We might more accurately say it attempts to redefine both "relations" and "content," as we see in the following passage written on November 25, 1860:

How is any scientific discovery made? Why, the discoverer takes it into his head first. He must all but see it.

I see several little white pines in Hosmer's meadow just beyond Lupine Hill, which must have sprung from seed which came some fifty rods,—probably blown so far in the fall. There are also a few in the road beyond Dennis's, which probably were blown from his swamp wood. So that there is nothing to prevent their springing up all over the village in a very few years—but our own plows and spades. They have also come up quite numerously in the young woodland north of J. P. B.'s Cold Pool (probably blown from the wood south of the pond), though they are evidently half a dozen years younger than the oaks there. I look at this large white pine wood by the pool to see if little ones come up under it. What was recently pasture comes up within a rod of this high wood on the north side, and, though the fence is gone, the different condition and history of the ground is very apparent by the different aspect of the little pines. There the old white pines are dense, and there are no little ones under them, but only a rod north they are very abundant, forming a dense thicket only two or three feet high bounded by a straight line on the south (or east and west), where the edge of the open land was within a rod of the great pines. Here they sprang up abundantly in the open land close by, but not at all under the pines. Yet within the great wood, wherever it is more open from any cause, I see a great many little pines springing up. Though they are thin and feeble comparatively, yet most of them will evidently come to be trees. White pines will spring up in the more open parts of a white pine wood, even under pines, though they are thin and feeble just in proportion to the density of the larger pines, and, where the large trees are quite dense, they will not spring up at all.

How commonly you see pitch pines, white pines, and birches filling up a pasture, and, when they are a dozen or fifteen years old, shrub and other oaks beginning to show themselves, inclosing apples trees and walls and fences gradually and so changing the whole aspect of the region. These trees do not cover the whole surface equally at present, but are grouped very agreeably after natural laws which they obey. You remember, perhaps, that fifteen years ago there was not a single tree in this pasture,—not a germinating seed of one,—and now it is a pretty dense forest ten feet high. I confess that I love to be convinced of this inextinguishable vitality in Nature. I would rather that my body should be buried in a soil thus wide-awake than in a mere inert and dead earth. (XIV:267–268)

The earth gives the pine trees life; the recognition of this proves its vitality, hence is exhilarating; the man making these observations desires his body to be buried in the same earth; in this final wish origins and ends, vitality and death, the life of the soil and the life of the vision impinge upon each other. Without compromising anything we know—that to be buried "in" nature is to be dead in and to it—the adjacencies I have described place something beside the knowledge. What they place beside it is the amplitude of the man's vision, the endlessness not of the man's life, but rather of his sight which, as it takes all this in, seems preternaturally to be possessed of the power to see in a glance the fifteen-year history of the "springing up" of these trees. The amount seen at once compensates for, and comes to seem equivalent to, seeing that would be continuous, in which the man, like the earth, would really be forever "wide-awake." The fiction of the *Journal* is that the breadth of the vision, and of visions like it, can be as if infinitely sustained, and that before this fact the knowledge that life has a duration is transient as a thought that only passes through the mind. The greatness of Thoreau's *Journal*, especially of its final volume, inheres in the way in which its lists and calculations (much like the assessments of the pine trees and the conditions of their growth) do not add up to nothing, do not dead-end in abstraction but transfigure their perceiver, add up to the exhilaration with which a passage like the one I have just cited almost routinely concludes. Then seeing nature outside the self does not objectify it, as seeing it inside the self does not familiarize it, for in Thoreau's *Journal* "seeing" is an intimate relation, not requisite for some other goal but an end in itself.

Walden's conclusion, formally so stipulated, implicitly promises immortal life, telling us in its last sentence, "The sun is but a morning star." The *Journal* has no conclusion. It ends at random six months prior to the death of its author, promising nothing of immortality, promising nothing but what it has already painstakingly delivered. In the *Journal* passage above, the suggestion that the life of the soil counters the death of the man stops short of the mysticism on which it verges, but we note in purely scientific terms that, although the man still dies, to be buried in soil "thus wide-awake" is to commit one's body to what "will evidently come to be trees" (a reversal of the transformation Thoreau had postulated when he asked about "what those solid trees have become"). In another *Journal* entry, he had triumphantly exclaimed, "The earth I see cannot bury me," and in the context of our considerations, we can understand such a proclamation to imply not just that seeing forestalls death, but that this earth—the one I see—regenerates what it buries, turns it over and back, obeys not the self's "inextinguishable vitality" but a larger "natural law" of its own.

"The greatest poverty," Wallace Stevens would note, comparatively ignorant about what he was speaking of, "is not to live in a physical world." Thoreau's *Journal* elucidates the statement, showing us what it might mean to rectify the deprivation. It is not a rectification we accept easily. For the greatest problem posed by the *Journal* is not in fact its length, albeit that is formidable. The greatest problem posed by the *Journal* is our wish not to be assaulted by its ideas as these are at once fearful and familiar: that meaning is not circumscribed; that we cannot excerpt it; that nature remains alien; that, notwithstanding, we continue to see it. In this respect *Walden* will remain the canonical text, as it converts those interminable *Journal* questions and illustrations to emblems, to recognitions, to codified meanings. My reader may, moreover, persist in believing that Thoreau kept this journal only as draft material for which he anticipated no publication. To imagine this to be the case, however, as I have implied, is further to vex our understanding of the *Journal* enterprise, for we must then wonder why during so much of his life, Thoreau treated draft material as primary writing. The issue of the *Journal*'s publication, however, while not inconsequential, is finally secondary. Especially to the extent that it deflects us from considering the less controvertible fact of the *Journal*'s composition, in which a man's passion for nature (intense, uncompromising, arguably obsessional) subordinates human presence, social conventions of order, that man's own literary reputation—all of the values to which we presume we aspire—to its own sustained, enviably unself-conscious, and absolutely forthright documentation.

NOTES

1. For a comprehensive account of the *Journal*'s publishing history, see the General Introduction to *Journal Volume 1: 1837–1844, The Writings of Henry David Thoreau,* ed. Elizabeth Witherell et al. (Princeton: Princeton University Press, 1981), pp. 578–591. See also the Textual Introduction to *Journal 1: 1837–1844.*

Forty-one intact manuscript notebooks are in the Pierpont Morgan library; one is in the Henry W. and Albert A. Berg Collection in the New York Public Library. Five other volumes, some numbered by Thoreau, some not, are being reconstructed from various sources by the Thoreau Edition editors. The question of numbering these volumes is tricky, and has occasioned confusion, since forty-two of the volumes are discretely bound while the remaining five volumes, so designated by the Textual Center, are only collections of now loose pages which will again become "books" only when they are reconstructed. Thoreau conceived of his *Journal* as its own coherent entity, *and* he appropriated passages from it to produce other, separate works. The latter practice accounts for the state of some of the texts, in which pages are physically separated from other pages and from a notebook as a whole. Thus while in *The New York Times Book Review* (December 20, 1981) Leon Edel complained that the Princeton Editors provided too much information about the appearance of the *Journal,* such information is crucial. If we think of Thoreau's *Journal* as a uniform entity, with all "volumes" consistently whole, we misconstrue the text.

2. The early *Journal* begins as a source book for literary quotation. (For a discussion of the years 1838 to 1844, see the Historical Introduction to *Journal 1* of the Princeton edition.) By May 31, 1850, Thoreau begins to write less sporadically in his *Journal.* By December 4, 1850, entries occur at several days' remove; in February of 1851, they are frequently penned on consecutive days. By June of 1851, Thoreau writes in his *Journal* almost every day—a practice that continues until November 3, 1861, when he is taken ill. The bulk of the volumes are composed, then, over a nine-year period. That bulk is considerable. Odell Shepard claims: "To speak of quantity alone, Emerson's 'Journals,' which cover a period of fifty-five years, are scarcely more than half as long as Thoreau's, which cover only twenty-four." (*The Heart of*

Thoreau's Journals [Boston: Houghton Mifflin, 1927], p. viii.) Stated as such this comparison is inaccurate. The Harvard edition of Emerson's *Journals and Miscellaneous Notebooks* tells us that the latter's journal is some three million words, compared to the two million of Thoreau's. The word count is still significant in light of the discrepancy between the number of years the two men wrote their respective works.

3. *The New Thoreau Handbook*, Walter Harding (New York: New York University Press, 1980). This book is indispensable for fleshing out questions of biography, as well as for information about Thoreau's works, his sources, his reading, and the Thoreau criticism. In addition, it directs readers to comprehensive bibliographies on these and other issues.

4. Harding, *Thoreau Handbook*, pp. xiii–xv.

5. There are obvious exceptions. On May 21, 1851, Thoreau concludes an entry by discussing the correspondence between names and their signified essences: "You have a wild savage in you, and a savage name is perchance somewhere recorded as yours" (5:438). Two days later he begins a new entry: "And wilder still there grows elsewhere I hear a native and aboriginal crabapple. . . ." It is, not coincidentally, in just this period—between 1850 and 1852—that Thoreau begins to regard the *Journal* as a continuous composition.

6. It is precisely because the *Journal* is a hybrid composition—not purely visually descriptive, literary, scientific, or philosophical—that it has thus far successfully resisted investigative procedures. Because the *Journal* appropriates features of disparate disciplines, it adheres neatly to the conventions of none of them.

Thus, for example, it is useful, to a point, to regard Thoreau as a natural historian. So John Hildebidle does in a fine recent study, *Thoreau: A Naturalist's Liberty* (Cambridge: Harvard University Press, 1983), which focuses on Thoreau's writings, mostly exclusive of the *Journal*, in the context of the genre of natural history. As Hildebidle notes, Thoreau had read Gilbert White's *Natural History of Selbourne* and Charles Darwin's *The Voyage of the Beagle*, and his work shares with theirs and with that of other natural historians a propensity to memorialize a specific place to which the self is subordinated. But Thoreau himself was dissatisfied with this description of his writing. Hence his insistence on the need to write a natural history "in a new sense." Perhaps most to the point, we cannot regard the *Journal* as a work of natural history, since one of its central presumptions, however fictional, is that no one is to be the beneficiary of the descriptions which are recorded. This presumption is opposite to that held by the natural historian, who writes to make his observations available to others.

7. *Consciousness in Concord: The Text of Thoreau's Hitherto Lost Journal (1840–1841)*, Perry Miller (Boston: Houghton Mifflin, 1958), p. 124.

8. After the above was written, Elizabeth Witherell suggested to me that the text from which Miller was working was a manuscript draft of an earlier version of "Life Without Principle." In other words, Witherell speculates that Miller was not looking at the *Journal* itself but at a later essay in which Thoreau himself incorporated part of the 1851 *Journal* entry:

> [Miller] dates [the passage] "before 1845" without giving any reason; two pieces of evidence suggest strongly that this is a draft for what was finally published as "Life Without Principle." The first is Miller's transcription of a "pencilled annotation" at the end: " 'What shall it profit etc.' " Thoreau's title for "Life Without Principle" when he gave it as a lecture for the fourth time, in Concord, February 17, 1855, was "What Shall it Profit?" The habit of keeping track of leaves of MS on which he was drafting lectures and essays by using catch phrases to lead from one to the next is characteristic with Thoreau; I think this is another example of that practice.
>
> The second piece of evidence is that parts of these paragraphs do appear in the *Journal* for 1851, in the 1906 edition as well as in our transcripts. Either Miller didn't know the *Journal* well enough to realize this or he chose not to mention it. Again, Thoreau's habit when drafting essays, lectures, and books, was to copy out passages from the *Journal*, lining through them in pencil in the MS volume of the *Journal* as he did so. It's not impossible that he would draft a passage on a loose leaf first and then copy it into the *Journal*, but it's highly unlikely. This passage in 7:82 is lined through with one of Thoreau's "use marks," and passages on the page before it and for several pages after it also show these use marks; some of the passages that follow survive to the final version of "Life Without Principle."
>
> I suggest that what Miller prints is part of a draft [of "Life Without Principle"], and that it dates from after September 7, 1851, perhaps as much later as late 1854, when Thoreau would

have been working on the first lecture version. . . . (From a letter dated June 5, 1984, by permission of the author.)

Witherell's speculation has since been confirmed by Bradley P. Dean, who identifies the manuscripts Miller quotes as part of the preliminary draft of the first lecture version of "Life Without Principle." Dean makes this identification in his master's thesis, "The Sound of a Flail: Reconstructions of Thoreau's Early 'Life Without Principle' Lectures" (Department of English, Eastern Washington University, Spring 1984).

The case, then, is an extreme but potentially illustrative one. Miller's sense of what characterizes the *Journal* (Thoreau's narcissism) allows him to find a passage that epitomizes the *Journal* that is not the *Journal*.

9. In the preface to *H. D. Thoreau: A Writer's Journal* (New York: Dover, 1960), Stapleton points to two crucial features of the *Journal*: that Thoreau's continued records of nature are not repetitions; that Thoreau's subject in the *Journal* is not "natural history" but is rather "relatedness" (p. xvi), specifically the relatedness "of lichen to rock, disintegrated rock to soil, soil to tree, tree to sky, and himself, a man, to each of these in each phase of change" (p. xvi). The space of a preface does not allow Stapleton to explore the meaning of the observations; perhaps as he does not regard the *Journal* as a discrete composition, he has nothing further to add to them. As my own reader will see, I think that both notions are central to our understanding of Thoreau, and that they require development.

10. What is notable about my claim that the *Journal* is central to Thoreau's writing is its profound *un*originality. But critics who have inevitably and correctly espoused this notion have mostly fallen back to discussing the *Journal* as the very draft material they had wished to claim it wasn't. Hence they have analyzed the *Journal* as a series of trial compositions; or as a composition subordinate to *Walden*, or as a work which, much like *Walden*, lacks the latter's organization. They have not considered the *Journal* as a discrete entity.

There are two exceptions—Perry Miller's *Consciousness in Concord* (1958), and William Howarth's *The Book of Concord: Thoreau's Life as a Writer* (New York: Viking, 1982)—but they are exceptions with provisos, for although each claims to talk about the work in its own right, he is differently diverted from doing so. Miller does not so much discuss the *Journal* as chastise Thoreau for writing it; Howarth treats the *Journal* as primary biographical evidence, not as composition.

11. I suppose one could conceive of Rousseau's *Reveries of a Solitary Walker* as presenting an opposite model. In that work, also published posthumously (we have no idea whether or not Thoreau read it), Rousseau claimed: "My enterprise is the same as Montaigne's, but my goal is the complete opposite of his: he wrote his *Essays* only for others, and I write my reveries only for myself. . . . I consecrate my last days to studying myself and to preparing in advance the account I will give of myself before long. Let me give myself up entirely to the sweetness of conversing with my soul." ("First Walk," trans. Charles E. Butterworth [New York: Harper Colophon ed., 1982].) Notwithstanding such protests, it is difficult to believe that Rousseau also did not intend his *Reveries* for posthumous publication.

12. *Walden*, ed. J. Lyndon Shanley (Princeton: Princeton University Press, 1971), p. 324. Further references in the text will be to this edition.

13. J. Lyndon Shanley, *The Making of Walden* (Chicago: University of Chicago Press, 1957), p. 30. In the Princeton edition of *Walden* which he has edited, Shanley makes the case most explicitly: "Thoreau did little if any work on *Walden* between 1849 and May 1851, but by early 1852 he had begun a far greater reworking of it than he had undertaken in his earlier revising" (p. 363). In May 1851, according to assertions of the *Journal,* it is interesting to note that Thoreau regarded *Walden* as substantially finished. Thus, for example, on May 6, 1851, he will write: "Like other preachers—I have added my texts—(derived from the Chinese and Hindoo scriptures)—long after my discourse was written" (5:411). I would argue, therefore, for Shanley's second date of "early 1852" for the resumption of work on *Walden.* Donald Ross, Jr. and Stephen Adams, in a more recent essay, "The Endings of *Walden* and the Stages of Its Composition" (*Research in the Humanities Bulletin* 84, 1981, 451–469) corroborate Shanley's findings that between 1850 and 1852 Thoreau did not substantially revise the *Walden* text. They also call attention to the crucial nature of the additions, emphasizing that it was not until the fifth stage, begun in 1852, that *Walden,* as we now know it, came into being.

Even allowing for Thoreau's return to writing *Walden* in early 1852, in the *Journal* entries for 1852—on January 22, 27, and 28, for example—Thoreau still speaks of the *Journal* (and journal discourse) as primary. On April 4, 1852, he refers to the *Journal* as the "source" of his life. Later, as I shall note, he calls the journal "the poet's only work" (October 21, 1857). Whatever the date for the resumption of

Walden, then, and I would argue it is the later of the two dates Shanley proposes, it is clear that the *Journal* remains for Thoreau a competitive, central task.

14. Shanley, *Making of Walden*, p. 56.

15. One could sensibly ask: when in 1852 Thoreau returned to serious revision of *Walden*, why did he abandon his hope for the *Journal*'s representation of nature? I would argue that he didn't. He merely came to see, in ways the subsequent pages will illustrate, the conflict between two exclusive impulses—to represent nature in its own right, and to present nature to an audience, to socialize the vision. *Walden* and the *Journal* each compromise one of these impulses. *Walden* betrays Thoreau's undivided attention to nature. The *Journal* betrays Thoreau's desire to bear witness. What Thoreau understood in 1852, then—or so I speculate—was the necessity for two, incompatible texts.

In light of these double contexts, I would say that some of the characteristics of *Walden* that Stanley Cavell first delineated in *The Senses of Walden* are most powerfully realized—have their native home—in Thoreau's *Journal*. It is not that these features could not logically apply to both *Walden* and the *Journal*, but rather that what is figurative in *Walden* (that, for example, the text is indifferent to a reader's presence) is literally true in the *Journal*. Certainly characteristics of the *Journal* (its investigation of nature as a radical enterprise) survive, in some measure, their translation to *Walden*. Cavell identifies these without, to my mind, acknowledging those properties of *Walden* (its literary self-consciousness, its elaborate provisions for an audience) that theatricalize and so jeopardize them.

16. Although this sentence follows a full two pages later, it only makes explicit what has been implied in the interim. For while Thoreau briefly entertains his question, considering the ways in which nature and his own reflections occupy the territory between one self and another, the meditation is repeatedly interrupted by digressions like the ones to which I point, whose content, in no uncertain terms, extols the value of solitude.

17. Over this matter-of-fact statement of division, critics have been unhappy. It may well be that the history of criticism of a given author reveals more about our own desires for what Emerson called "The Uses of Great Men" than it does about the work in its own right. Then the history of Thoreau criticism would be a testament to the nostalgia for

the reconciliation of men with other men, the social world with the natural one. So Stanley Cavell in *The Senses of Walden* (New York: Viking, 1972), and earlier, Sherman Paul in *The Shores of America* (Urbana: University of Illinois Press, 1958), are at pains to show the ways in which Thoreau speaks for the human community by teaching us our own natures. So, oppositely, but also goaded by the impulse to demonstrate the proper unity of the natural and the human, Richard Bridgman, in *Dark Thoreau* (Lincoln: University of Nebraska Press, 1982), rebukes Thoreau for betraying the human for the natural. So Perry Miller, in *Consciousness in Concord*, is incensed at the self-sabotage of this betrayal. Other studies have insisted that although Thoreau's allegiance to the human and his allegiance to the natural may not simultaneously be espoused, they are nonetheless complementary. I take this to be the position of Frederick Garber's *Thoreau's Redemptive Imagination* (New York: New York University Press, 1977), as well as of James McIntosh's *Thoreau as Romantic Naturalist* (Ithaca: Cornell University Press, 1974), concentrating, as both do, on Thoreau's ambivalence toward nature, and therefore on attitudes of his which cannot be separated or opposed precisely because they are protean. However different (in the case of Cavell and Bridgman, however opposite) their respective stands, these critics have a stake in characterizing Thoreau's allegiance to the social and the natural as compatible, or in taking him to task because they are not compatible, or in blurring the issue of compatibility by focusing on ambivalence. They have a stake in extolling Thoreau for a position he does not (here) hold, or in upbraiding him for not extolling it, or in reconciling the conflict between approbation and disapproval—and in reconciling, too, the conflict between the natural or the social by observing the ways in which Thoreau navigates between them. They have a stake in disregarding the alternatives specified as exclusive.

18. "Thoreau's Journals," Alfred Kazin (*New York Herald Tribune Books*, 1951).

19. I would argue here with the idea espoused by Perry Miller in "Thoreau in the Context of International Romanticism" (*The New England Quarterly* 34:2, June, 1961, 147–59) that Thoreau is not writing about nature but is rather "projecting . . . emotions onto the natural setting." In the passages at which we have looked, this is exactly what Thoreau is not doing.

In a sentence of the same essay, Miller implicitly, and importantly, touches on the significance of Thoreau's use of analogy, but the description which follows does not take account of the subversion of analogic conventions which we have been considering. Thus Miller faults Thoreau for the belief that "moral law and natural law contain analogies, and that, for this reason the writer may safely record facts without metaphors, since truths are bound to sprout from them." *Walden* may be predicated on the assumption of such an analogic relationship; the *Journal* is predicated on the antithesis of this assumption. If in the *Journal* natural data are unexplained, this is not because Thoreau assumes human meanings will "sprout" from them. Explanation is absent because there is no mediating ground for it.

Although on May 20, 1851, Thoreau writes: "There is no doubt a perfect analogy between the life of the human being and that of the vegetable," the remainder of the entry suggests he is going through the motions of demonstrating analogic equivalence. As we have seen, removed from abstraction, and from the pedagogic imperative to produce correspondences, contemplation of nature bereaves the mind of natural counterparts.

20. My position differs from Porte's in this essential way: Thoreau relinquishes a belief in correlatives between nature and the mind not because he has no interest in them, but rather because, as I have argued, he finds them persistently unavailable.

21. "*Walden*'s False Bottoms," *Glyph* I, 1977, 132–49.

22. In *The Senses of Walden*, Stanley Cavell points out that in *Walden* "Our relation to nature, at its best would be neighboring. . . ." (p. 103). Cavell's observation is, in fact, faithful to Thoreau's own juxtaposition of human neighborhoods which are insignificant and natural atmospheres which are sustaining. But Thoreau's word-play notwithstanding, I would argue that in *Walden* Thoreau's relation to nature is appropriative and proprietary rather than proximate. In *Walden*, living in nature means reaping its meanings as in "the hoeing of beans to serve a parable maker."

23. Hence the vigilance which clocks phenomena from one year to the next: "I see again the same kinds of clouds that I saw the 10th of last April" (March 30, 1853). As the April 18 entry of 1852, at which we have been looking, documents the appearance of catkins which are the first sign of spring, so on March 10, 1853, Thoreau observes that the bloom of the catkins predates that of the previous year. On May 8, 1853 (V:140), we are told that to mark the occurrence of a natural

phenomenon is to discover territory heretofore uncharted: "This then is the very earliest date of robin-plaintain. Neither of these did I see last year, and I was affected as if I had got into a new botanical district." In fact, the year 1853, more than any other *Journal* year, is particularly concerned with the first appearance of phenomena and with cross-checkings to previous years. Perhaps this is because Thoreau is there becoming conscious of the complicated relation between the repetition of an event and its permutations. "If you make the least correct observation of nature this year," Thoreau writes on April 7, 1853 (V:100), "you will have occasion to repeat it with illustrations the next, and the season and life itself is prolonged." Consolation comes not from the idea that a phenomenon will be replicated but rather from the idea that man will again be granted the opportunity to see a similar phenomenon with accuracy, for to see something twice is to see it with a difference:

> These spring impressions (as of the apparent waking up of the meadow described day before yesterday) are not repeated the same year, at least not with the same force, for the next day the same phenomenon does not surprise us. Our appetite has lost its edge. The other day the face of the meadow wore a peculiar appearance, as if it were beginning to wake up under the influence of the southwest wind and the warm sun, but it cannot again this year present precisely that appearance to me. I have taken a step forward to a new position and must see something else. (March 18, 1858 [X:307])

24. I here intend the sexism of my language. It accurately reflects Thoreau's. It is men, not women, for whom he expresses regard.

25. *Henry David Thoreau*, Joseph Wood Krutch, American Men of Letters series (New York: William Sloane Associates, 1948), p. 227.

26. In Miller's vitriolic words from *Consciousness in Concord*: "Emerson, Margaret Fuller, the 'lesser' Transcendentalists, but above all Thoreau, devoted a dismaying proportion of their energies to attesting the paradox that the more they loved each other, the more they could do without each other" (p. 89). Miller further complains about the "insatiable drive" that produces "rhetorical devices" in the *Journal* after 1850 for "translating friendship into no friendship" (p. 90).

27. Miller, *Consciousness in Concord*, p. 25.

28. Whatever the failings of Perry Miller's monograph, it is without question the best study of the *Journal* and, to my mind, one of the most tangentially interesting comments on American Transcendentalism. While it is fashionable to write this essay off as a product of Miller's age, the essay demonstrates an exacting analysis of Thoreau's *Journal* and of Thoreau's work in general, unblinded by pieties about man's love of nature. It is just because Miller seems not to be confronting sentiments or material in any way alien that what he has to say is undistracted by rhetorical postures of adulation. This familiarity is at once responsible for opinions that manhandle the *Journal*, rough it up with disapproval, and for that straightforward explication of, even sympathy for, Thoreau's major work. In the single comment that Thoreau's *Journal* to be read at all must be read whole, Perry Miller makes an inestimable contribution; his remark alerts us to the fact that we are dealing with a "literary performance."

29. The *Journal* may not literally be free of notations about daily events or about persons, but in the context of the major object of scrutiny—nature—these notations seem trivial, marginal, almost always subordinate. Sometimes Thoreau provides information that promises to be personal, while withholding the elaboration that would explain what—as given—is only abstract or cryptic. For example, on December 26, 1855, Thoreau catalogues, without commenting upon, the houses in which he lived (as well as the dates of his occupancy), a list of his writings, and other important events during the time of his residencies. Such an entry invites us to consider the relation between dates, houses, events, and significance attributed to their relation. But significance—especially any explanation of emotional significance—is just what is missing. However unintentionally, this is provocative, since the sentence which precedes the chronology seems to promise to rectify the lack of documentation it is describing: "I find in my Journal that the most important events in my life, if recorded at all, are not dated." (VIII:64).

30. In *Walden* this doubleness takes the form of a conscious self that regards its own actions: "However intense my experience, I am conscious of the presence and criticism of part of me, which, as it were, is not part of me, but spectator, sharing no experience . . . When the play, it may be the tragedy, of life is over, the spectator goes his way." What is notable is the theatrical image in which *Walden* describes such doubleness, and also—in distinction from the *Journal*—that the point of the doubleness is not to direct attention outward but

rather to make it self-referential. I take these two impulses—attention to oneself and theatricalizing the fate of that self—to be related.

31. Brackets in the quotation are my own.

32. It would be easy to embark on a long digression and to argue that Shelley's "Ode" is in fact representative of the differences between the beliefs espoused by the Thoreau of the *Journal* and those espoused by the British Romantics in general. I will settle for a footnote which suggests, without elaborating, the characteristic features of the Shelley poem I have discussed. For pointing me to several of my examples, I am indebted to Jerome Christensen.

It is true, of course, that Wordsworth, in the "Preface to *Lyrical Ballads*," espouses the value of ordinary language and ordinary experience. Moreover, he insists, nature exemplifies these. But what nature exemplifies for Wordsworth is in fact *human* sentiments. Hence, although the leech-gatherer looks like a "stone," what entices Wordsworth about that fact is the ease with which the speaker can read human meanings "on" (from) the man, can "espy" not nature but rather strength that, human, he can learn to make his own. Hence, although in "The Solitary Reaper," the woman's inscrutable song is compared to that of the nightingale or the cuckoo, and, like theirs, resists translation, all the guesses about the song's theme speculate human concerns. Hence in "Essay on Epitaphs" we are told those epitaphs are best in which the dead speak in their own persons, for in those cases utterance is founded on "a solid basis," that is, it is founded on rock which preserves human powers. (This is exactly contrary to Thoreau's preference, for when Thoreau says he wants to write sentences "which lie like boulders across the page," what he means to write are sentences *empty* of human affect.) Finally, when in Wordsworth's work the self *is* naturalized, naturalization is what happens to someone else, as in the "Lucy" poems.

So, too, Keats imagines oneness with nature—fusion with the nightingale—as equivalent to the death he at once courts and shies away from, and we could say the poem ends to prevent the self's very conversion into song that it initially solicits. In fact, the tension of much of Keats's poetry enacts the double movement I describe—the desire for self-transcendence (the wish to leave the self behind and to be naturalized or transported) and, recoiling from this impulse, the terror of doing so. The only viable solution to the wish to escape "the weariness, the fever and the [human] fret" and the countering fear that the self will be caught in an unrecognizable nowhere, whether this be in the stalled movement of the figures on the urn, the abandonment of "La Belle Dame" or the inhuman grandeur before which the two "Hyperion" poems fragment, is that oblivion which will blur, and momentarily reconcile, the competitive desires, as at the end of "Ode on Melancholy." Another way to put this is to say Keats is reluctant to feel the empathy about which he frequently speaks. Thus he writes to Benjamin Bailey on November 22, 1817: " . . . if a sparrow come before my window I take part in its existence and pick about the gravel." But in articulating this identification, he also recoils from it, saying, "I suspect myself and these feelings . . . thinking them a few barren tragedy tears," that is, distrusting them as theatrical.

Of all the British Romantics, Coleridge's attitudes toward nature are perhaps closest to Thoreau's, although it is interesting to note that Coleridge's *Notebooks* illustrate a progression opposite to that in the *Journal*. The early notebooks read like accretions of uncommented-upon natural detail; as they progress, however, Coleridge aestheticizes them, making them into a symbology or composition. In Thoreau's *Journal*, as I shall discuss, the aesthetic concerns which mark the early volumes are later winnowed to a record of unencumbered detail.

33. In those infrequent *Journal* entries in which Thoreau seems to imagine a contemporary audience for the *Journal*, the tone becomes didactic: "Let me say to you and myself in one breath—cultivate the tree which you have found to bear fruit in your soil. Regard not your past failures nor successes . . ." (3:187). Didacticism apparently precipitated by the mere idea of addressing others is reminiscent of the pontificating moments that assault us in *Walden*, for example, from its "Conclusion": "However mean your life is, meet it and live it; do not shun it and call it hard names. It is not so bad as you are."

34. In insisting upon this distinction, I would nonetheless be arguing with Mary Elkins Moller, who in *Thoreau in the Human Community* (Amherst: University of Massachusetts Press, 1980) attempts to rescue Thoreau from the charge of man-hating, first by pointing out the number and adequacy of Thoreau's actual friendships, and secondly by insisting that Thoreau's misanthropy is rooted in idealism (p. 137). Neither Thoreau's love of mankind nor his hatred of mankind—as these attitudes are recorded—are separable (at least with respect to their utterance in the *Journal*) from Thoreau's desire to create a discourse wholly self-sufficient in which the self can be the audience for the nature it has internalized, can be, at least fictionally, its own first

and second person. Thus I wish to suggest that studies which see Thoreau as an affirmer of men (Sherman Paul's), or as a rejecter of men (Perry Miller's, Richard Bridgman's), as a man whose negations are based on affirmations (Mary Elkins Moller's), present incomplete postulates. With respect to the *Journal*, each fails to consider these attitudes in the context that would orient them—the others, or outsiders, the immediate (external) audience which would deflect Thoreau's attention from the object of his contemplation.

35. In the essay on friendship in the "Wednesday" chapter of *A Week on the Concord and Merrimack Rivers,* Thoreau may point to the discrepancy between friendship's reality and its ideal ("Friendship is as evanescent in every man's experience, and remembered like heat lightning in past summers") but the thrust of the essay is to heal the breach which elicits comment. So the sentence which follows the previous one maintains: "Fair and flitting like a summer cloud—there is always some vapor in the air no matter how long the drought." The *Journal,* in contrast, consistently adumbrates the notion of discrepancy: "I was never so near my friend when he was bodily present as when he was absent" (2:33), and "Can it be that my friend is but a suggestion & hint of a friend whom I have never seen. . . . I see too plainly that if I degraded my ideal to an identity with any actual mortal whose hand is to be grasped there would be an end of our fine relations. I would be related to my friend by the most etherial part of our natures alone" (2:34).

36. Again, as the passages to which I have pointed imply, the sexism of my language is faithful to Thoreau's. In Perry Miller's facetious and—I think—accurate words: "Thoreau flouted the highest, the most sacred, duty of masculinity: he was not interested in women" (Miller, p. 81).

37. If we assume that Thoreau intended the *Journal* for publication, we could say that the structure of its entries would betray an attitude toward its readers. We might gauge that attitude by inferring how a given entry seemed implicitly to imagine, and implicitly to fulfill or frustrate, a reader's expectations. In raising the questions of expectations we are of course on tentative ground, because expectations apply to works whose authors intend their publication. Journal discourse disqualifies the idea of expectations because journals are ostensibly "private," hence presume the "non-existence of hearers."

38. Miller, *Consciousness in Concord,* p. 32.

39. Thoreau would have absorbed an interest in the dialogue between science and poetry from numerous contemporary sources—from Darwin and Linnaeus; from the British Romantics (particularly Wordsworth and Coleridge); from his reading of Goethe; from direct contact with Asa Gray and Louis Agassiz—quite simply, and in ways impossible to document in their entirety, from the culture in which he was living. One source, however, may bear special examination: Coleridge's conciliation of science and poetry. We can only guess at whether Thoreau saw similarities between Coleridge's attempt to conjoin science and poetry and his own efforts to reconcile them. Attempting his own synthesis, he would write on August 1, 1860: "How much of beauty, of color as well as form, on which our eyes daily rest goes unperceived by us. No one but a botanist is likely to distinguish nicely the different shades of green with which the open surface of the earth is clothed—not even a landscape painter if he does not know the species of sedges and grasses which paint it."

Although Thoreau at times disparages men of science who make meaning of such calculations, he is, as I have noted, equally quick to discredit William Gilpin—the English landscape writer—calling the latter's treatment of nature a mere aesthetic composition. He complains of Ruskin's *Modern Painters:* "I am disappointed in not finding it a more out-of-door book. . . . He does not describe nature as Nature, but as Turner painted her" (October 6, 1857 [X:69]).

Index

170 WRITING NATURE

as subject, 128–132
substituted for plot, 109, 132, 139, 151
In the Woods and Fields of Concord: Selections from the Journals of Henry David Thoreau, 21

Journal. See also Journal and Walden; Thoreau, Henry David
abstraction in, 59, 140–41
accessibility of, 3, 83, 92, 103, 125, 154
aesthetics in, 111, 114, 145, 166
anthologies of, 21, 25. *See also Journal*, problems of interpretation in, quotation from
anthropocentrism in, 11, 12, 13, 66, 68, 76, 90, 114, 147–48
audience for, 16, 26, 80–85, 90–96, 98–108, 167. *See also* Audience: *Journal*, posthumous publication and audience
as autonomous composition, 6, 16, 22, 25, 151, 154, 158, 164
as composition of nature, 21, 88, 114, 117, 129
criticism of, 17–21, 91, 103, 108, 158. *See also individual critics*
discontinuity in, 4, 6, 15–17, 62, 84, 149. *See also Journal*, fragmentation in; *Journal*, problems of interpretation, disorder; Relations
documentation in, 61, 144, 154. *See also Journal*, as history and record of nature
as draft material. *See Journal*, as autonomous composition
editions of, ix, 3, 18, 155. *See also individual editions (title or publisher) and editors*
as effort to read nature, 12, 21, 31, 72–73, 112
exemplification in, 10, 17, 78, 109–117, 128–32, 137
and figurative language, 32, 34, 42–48, 72–74, 80, 163. *See also Journal*, rhetorical strategies in, analogy
analogy, 11, 27, 32, 37–48, 65–75, 149–51, 161–62

metaphor, 13–14, 41, 45, 53, 65, 72–74, 85, 111, 149
subversion of, 38–48, 65, 68–74, 107, 132, 141, 149
symbolization, 45, 47, 58–59, 61–63, 132
synedoche, 78, 109
focus in, 9, 13, 15, 57, 67, 114, 125, 128–30. *See also Journal*, problems of interpretation in, difficulty of determining subject; *Journal*, problems of interpretation in, multiple foci
fragmentation in, 6, 16, 66, 92. *See also Journal*, discontinuity in
as guide to its own interpretation, 4, 10, 66, 68, 106
as history and record of nature, 9–11, 15, 88, 94, 103, 109, 129, 148, 156–57
the human and the natural in, 8–9, 11–14, 25–26, 31–37, 46, 69, 77–79, 88–93, 112–114, 128–29, 137, 145–51, 154, 161. *See also* Nature; Self
human relations in, 5, 28, 84, 93, 95–101, 103, 163, 166, 167. *See also* Relations, intimate; Thoreau, aversion to society
idea of totality in, 6, 74, 105, 129, 136
indices of, 64, 110
light in, 12–13, 112, 126–28, 136–37, 145
and literal language, 74, 101
as literary work, 26, 47–48, 61, 80, 82, 93, 102–103, 105, 140, 159, 165
manuscript volumes of, 3, 9, 17–19, 21, 64, 134–37. 149, 155
marginalization of the human in, 5, 11–12, 23, 31, 46, 57, 66, 75, 85, 88–93, 111, 145–46, 149, 151. *See also* Thoreau, aversion to society
mind and nature in, 16, 35–38, 42–45, 60, 67–68, 87–88, 130–34, 148–153, 162
morality of nature in, 33, 45, 57–62
mythology in, 26, 58, 78, 86, 149
naming in, 20, 62–66, 72–78, 98,